AQA

REVISE AQA GCSE
English and English Language

REVISION GUIDE

Foundation

Series Consultant: Harry Smith

Author: David Grant

- -

Also available to support your revision:

Revise GCSE Study Skills Guide   9781447967071

The **Revise GCSE Study Skills Guide** is full of tried-and-trusted hints and tips for how to learn more effectively. It gives you techniques to help you achieve your best – throughout your GCSE studies and beyond!

Revise GCSE Revision Planner   9781447967828

The **Revise GCSE Revision Planner** helps you to plan and organise your time, step-by-step, throughout your GCSE revision. Use this book and wall chart to mastermind your revision.

For the full range of Pearson revision title
BTEC and AS Level visit:

www.pearsonschools.co.uk/revise

ALWAYS LEARNING

PEARSON

Contents

A small bit of small print

AQA publishes Sample Assessment Material and the Specification on its website. This is the official content and this book should be used in conjunction with it. The questions in **Now try this** have been written to help you practise every topic in the book. Remember: the real exam questions may not look like this.

Questions 1 and 2

Before you get stuck into your revision for Section A: Reading, you need to know:

- ☑ **what sort of questions you will be answering**
- ☑ how long you will have to spend on each answer
- ☑ how to pick out the key information in the question.

In Section A, you will have to read **three** unseen source texts and answer **five** questions. This page covers Questions 1 and 2. Don't try to answer the exam questions on this page – just get used to the style.

Question 1 is in **two parts**. It tests your ability to **retrieve, understand** and **interpret** information from the first text, **Source 1.**

This means picking out relevant pieces of information that answer the **two** questions.

It tests the following assessment objective:

> Read and understand texts, selecting material appropriate to purpose, collating from different sources and making comparisons and cross-references as appropriate.

This is an example of Question 1.

This is the opening of an example of Source 1.

Source 1

Supermarkets are killing us

Shetland's dairy farmers say their farms are facing an uncertain future as

1 (a) List **four** problems facing dairy farmers in the Shetland Islands. *(4 marks)*

1 (b) What do you learn about the farmers' reactions to the problems they face? *(4 marks)*

Question 2 tests your ability to **understand and interpret meaning** in the second text, **Source 2.**

This means identifying or inferring, and explaining information relevant to the question.

It tests the following assessment objective:

> Read and understand texts, selecting material appropriate to purpose, collating from different sources and making comparisons and cross-references as appropriate.

This is the opening of an example of Source 2.

Source 2

Confessions of a stuntman

One of the most dangerous and hair-raising escapades of my career came when I was asked to

This is an example of Question 2.

2 What problems did Steve Bray face after this stunt? Remember to:
- show your understanding by explaining in your own words
- support your ideas using the text. *(8 marks)*

Now try this

Answer the following questions using the information on this page.

1 What skill will Question 1 of your exam test you on?

2 What skill will Question 2 of your exam test you on?

1

Questions 3 and 4

Before you get stuck into your revision for Section A: Reading, you need to know:

- ☑ **what sort of questions you will be answering**
- ☑ how long you will have to spend on each answer
- ☑ how to pick out the key information in the question.

In Section A, you will have to read **three** unseen source texts and answer **five** questions. This page covers Questions 3 and 4. Don't try to answer the exam questions on this page – just get used to the style.

Question 3 tests your ability to write about **the effectiveness of language** in **Source 3**.

This means identifying language features, and commenting closely on their effect.

It tests both of the assessment objectives at once.

> Read and understand texts, selecting material appropriate to purpose, collating from different sources and making comparisons and cross-references as appropriate.

This is the opening of an example of Source 3.

Source 3

Foods of the future
Growing population and dwindling resources may mean a major re-think of what we are prepared to eat

This is an example of Question 3.

3 How does the writer use **language features** to inform the reader and **persuade** them to change their eating habits?
Remember to:
- give some examples of language features to inform
- give some examples of language features to persuade
- explain the effects.   *(12 marks)*

Question 4 tests your ability to write about **presentational features** and **compare texts**. This means commenting closely on how the two texts are presented and the effect on the reader.

It tests both of the assessment objectives at once.

> Explain and evaluate how writers use linguistic, grammatical, structural and presentational features to achieve effects and engage and influence the reader, supporting your comments with detailed textual references.

This is an example of Question 4.

4 Look again at **Source 1** and **Source 3**. Compare the way that **both** texts use **presentational features** for effect. Remember to:
- write about the way the sources are presented
- explain the effect of the presentational features
- compare the way they **look**.   *(12 marks)*

When answering this question you will be asked to refer to **two** of the texts that you have looked at for Questions 1, 2 and 3.

Now try this

Answer the following questions using the information on this page.
1 What skill will Question 3 of your exam test you on?
2 What skill will Question 4 of your exam test you on?

Planning your time in the exam

Before you get stuck into your revision for Section A: Reading, you need to know:

✓ what sort of questions you will be answering

✓ **how long you will have to spend on each answer**

✓ how to pick out the key information in the question.

Running out of time is one of the most common ways that students lose marks in their exam. You should plan your time to get the most out of every minute. This page will help you prepare for this.

The English/English Language Unit I exam is 2 hours and 15 minutes long.

Section A, Reading is worth 40 marks.

Section B, Writing is worth 40 marks.

You should spend:

* 15 minutes reading the source texts for Section A, Reading
* I hour answering the questions in Section A, Reading
* I hour answering the questions in Section B, Writing.

See page 53

for more on planning for Section B: Writing

The first 15 minutes

You should spend the first 15 minutes of the exam reading the source texts and the questions you will be asked about them. So when you are told that you may start, you could:

1 **Read the questions** to find out what you're looking for when you read the source texts.

2 **Skim read the source texts** to get a rough idea of what they are about and the main ideas.

3 **Read the source texts carefully**, thinking about the information, ideas, and presentational and language features that you will write about.

4 **Read Question I again, then go through Source I**, highlighting information and ideas that will help you answer the question.

5 **Do the same for Question 2** and **Source 2**, then **Question 3** and **Source 3**.

6 **Decide which two texts you will write about in Question 4**, then go through them highlighting relevant features.

See page 7

for more on annotating sources

Worked example

Work out how long to spend on Question 1 in the **Section A**, **Reading** exam paper.

The Section A exam lasts I hour, or 60 minutes, and is worth 40 marks. That gives me 1½ minutes for every mark. So if Question I (a) is worth 4 marks, I should spend 6 minutes answering it.

Now try this

Now work out how long you need to spend on Questions 1 (b) *(4 marks)*, 2 *(8 marks)*, 3 *(12 marks)* and 4 *(12 marks)*, in minutes.

To check your answer, add all the times for all five questions together – they should add up to 60 (minutes).

Reading the questions

Before you get stuck into your revision for Section A: Reading, you need to know:

☑ what sort of questions you will be answering

☑ how long you will have to spend on each answer

☑ **how to pick out the key information in the question.**

You need to read each question on the exam paper very carefully to make sure you know exactly what it is asking you to do. This page will help you practise how to focus on the key words in questions. Don't try to answer the exam questions on this page – just focus on picking out the key words.

Read **Source 1.**

1 (a) List **four** problems facing dairy farmers in the Shetland Islands?
  (4 marks)

Check which source you are being asked to write about.

Check the focus of the question – that is, the information and ideas you are being asked to write about.

How many pieces of information are you being asked to find?

---

2 What problems did Steve Bray face after this stunt?
  Remember to:
  • show your understanding by explaining in your own words
  • support your ideas using the text.
  (8 marks)

Pick out the key words in the question. Make sure you focus only on the information you are asked to write about.

Make sure you **explain** the information and give examples from the text.

You must describe these features and **explain** how they are **effective**.

---

3 How does the writer use **language features** to **inform** the reader and **persuade** them to change their eating habits?
  Remember to:
  • give some examples of language features to inform
  • give some examples of language features to persuade
  • explain the effects. *(12 marks)*

Make sure you know what the question is asking you to focus on – and make sure you don't write about anything else.

Pick out the key words in the question and make sure you use them to answer the question.

You will need to give examples and **explain** them.

Now try this

4 Look again at **Source 1** and **Source 3.**
  Compare the way that **both** texts use **presentational features** for effect.
  Remember to:
  • write about the way the sources are **presented**
  • explain the **effect** of the presentational features
  • compare the way they **look.** *(12 marks)*

Now you need to refer to **Source 1** and **Source 3.**
You are going to compare the **two** texts.
Look at this exam question.
• Which source texts should you write about?
• What are the keywords in the question that tell you what to do?
• What feature of the texts is this question asking you to write about?
• What does the question advise you to do when writing your answer?
• How many marks is this question worth?
• How long should you spend writing your answer to this question?

Approaching the exam paper

Once you're in the exam hall, you need to get to work as soon as you turn over the exam paper. This page will show you how to put what you've learned over the last four pages into practice. Don't try to answer these exam questions – just focus on picking out key information and working out how long you can spend on each question.

For each question make sure you identify **exactly** what the question is asking you to do. Look at Question 1 below to see how you can identify all the important information in the question.

✓ Identifies how many things to list from the source text.

✓ Identifies key focus of question.

Section A: Reading
Answer **all** questions in this section.
You are advised to spend about one hour on this section.

Read **Source 1**.

1 **(a)** List **four** things you learn about Barry Barnes.   *(4 marks)*

1 **(b)** What do you learn from **Source 1** about the ways in which Barry Barnes's early life has affected his health?   *(4 marks)*

✓ Identifies which source text to write about.

✓ Highlights two areas to look for in the source text.

Now read **Source 2**.

2 What made Shane Ridley want to become a computer game designer?
Remember to:
• show your understanding by explaining in your own words
• support your ideas using the text.   *(8 marks)*

Timing plan
Reading the question and
source texts   (9.00–9.15am)
Q1 (a): 6 mins   (9.15–9.21am)
Q1 (b): 6mins   (9.21–9.27am)
Q2: 12 mins   (9.27–9.39am)
Q3
Q4

Now read **Source 3**.

3 How does the writer use **language features** to **describe** the situation and **persuade** the reader to make a donation?
Remember to:
• give some examples of language features to describe
• give some examples of language features to persuade
• explain the effects.   *(12 marks)*

4 Look again at **Source 1** and **Source 3**. **Compare** the way that **both** texts use **presentational features** for effect.
Remember to:
• write about the way the sources are **presented**
• explain the **effect** of the presentational features
• compare the way they **look**.   *(12 marks)*

Now try this

1 Look at the timing plan above. Complete the plan for Questions 3 and 4.

2 Look at the way that the key information has been picked out of Question 1. Now pick out the key features of Questions 2, 3 and 4.

Make sure you identify:
• which source to write about
• the key focus of the question
• what you are being asked to write about.

Skimming for the main idea

Time is precious in the exam so it's a good idea to skim-read the source text before reading it in detail. This will give you a good idea of what the text is about.

Key features

Look at these key places when you skim-read a text.

The heading.

The first sentence of each paragraph.

The last sentence of the text.

Summing up

Think about how you would sum up the entire article in one sentence. Here are two possibilities for the article on the right:

- Britain wastes a lot of money on tidying up litter.
- Litter is expensive.

Britain's 'litter epidemic' costs almost £1bn every year

A Keep Britain Tidy survey shows the cost of employing litter pickers and buying equipment to clear chewing gum rose by £100 million in the last year.

The Local Government Association said it was 'environmental vandalism' that is robbing councils of money to pay for schools and hospitals.

The chief executive of Keep Britain Tidy said, 'it is quite obscene that we, as a nation, have to spend more than £¾ billion clearing up the rubbish that people can't be bothered to put in a bin'.

Now try this

Look at this newspaper article for 20 seconds. How could you sum it up in **one** sentence?

Remember to look at:
- the headline
- the first sentence of each paragraph
- the last sentence of the article.

Not alone: the importance of helping victims of cyberbullying

More than one in three young people in the UK have been a victim of cyberbullying. One in 13 suffers from persistent abuse online. That abuse is cruel, invasive and intimidating.

And the results can be devastating. The rapid development of technology means many of the barriers that arguably acted as deterrents to traditional bullying have been removed. Cyberbullies often feel empowered by the belief they are anonymous and feel sheltered by the false view they are safe from the repercussions of their actions.

Young people rightly want to know what 'we' are going to do about it. It is time for us to be clear about where responsibility lies. Research shows that young people have the power and the desire to change the culture of the online world in which they now live, but it is now up to us as society to lead the way.

Annotating the sources

Get used to highlighting, underlining or circling parts of a source that you can use to support your answers.

Highlight and annotate

Look at this question.

> **3** How does the writer use **language features** to **describe** and **inform** the reader?
>
> Remember to:
> * give some examples of language features to inform
> * give some examples of language features to describe
> * explain the effects.   *(12 marks)*

Source 1

'I used to hate weightlifting but I've grown to love it'

The noise is terrifying. Eeeeeyaaaahah. Crash. Aaaaaaaaaaaaaaeugh! Thud. Close your eyes and you could be in a war zone. Open them, and it doesn't get much better. A man with a tiny belted waist and pumped muscles twists his face into an agonising gurn, lifts the bar above his head, and lets it fall. The weights explode on to the floor like fireworks.

Emotive language – shows the writer feels frightened.

Emphasises pain and fear.

Suggests weightlifters are very fit and strong.

Sounds dangerous but spectacular – simile.

Don't just highlight useful quotes. Note down:
* the effect on the reader
* the technique used to achieve it.

Now try this

Read the next paragraph of the newspaper article. Highlight any words or phrases from this text that you could use to answer the exam-style question above.

Look for words and phrases that either **inform** or **describe**.

Here in the gym at Leeds Metropolitan University, British weightlifters are training for the Olympics. They are an extraordinarily dedicated bunch of athletes. They have to be. The British team have given up their jobs or studies to survive on £100 a week from UK Sport, there are no cash prizes for winning, and few sponsorship deals. Training is torture, their hands are callused and blistered, and they know they have next to no chance of winning medals. But that's not the point.

Selecting information

Question 1 (a) tests your ability to **retrieve** information from a source text.

You need to pick out and use **only the information that is relevant** to the question.

Look at this question.

> 1 (a) List **four** things you learn from **Source 1** about Suzanne Collins.   *(4 marks)*

To answer it you need to pick out relevant information about Collins herself. Look at these examples:

These tell you about Collins herself.

These tell you about her book and the film of her book.

> Note that the question asks about the author, so this information is not relevant.

Source 1

Suzanne Collins: Hunger Games author

There are many bestselling children's authors but only rarely do any break through into the universal cultural consciousness. Now along comes Suzanne Collins, a 49-year-old from Connecticut, in the USA, with The Hunger Games trilogy.

It's too early to know how durable this series will prove, but the signs so far are good. It has spent more than 100 weeks on the New York Times bestseller list. The film has made converts of even the most curmudgeonly critics, grossing more than \$531m (£327m) worldwide in its first four weeks. More than 1m copies of the books are now in print in the UK, and last month Amazon announced that Collins had become the bestselling Kindle author so far.

Now try this

Read the next paragraph of the article about Suzanne Collins. List **three** things you learn about her from this paragraph. Select relevant information.

Remember to:
- select information that will help you answer the question
- ignore information that will not.

The woman behind the phenomenon is a bit of a mystery. She is married to a TV actor, but she doesn't do publicity, and hasn't even met her UK publishers. Is her reluctance to self-publicise innocent or knowing? Either way, it's striking in the context of The Hunger Games, which is set in a nation, Panem, in which everything is televised. A fragmented post-apocalyptic society is ruled by the fascistic Capitol, which keeps the masses quiet by feeding them reality war games featuring teenagers who must fight to the last one standing.

Purpose and audience

The first things you should think about when you read a text are its purpose and its audience.

Purpose

The purpose of a text is the reason why it was written. Texts can do any of these things:
- describe
- explain
- inform
- advise
- argue
- persuade
- review
- analyse

Audience

The audience of a text is who the text is aimed at. A writer might aim their text at an audience:
- of men, or women or both
- from a particular age group or age range
- with particular interests.

Worked example

1 (a) What do you learn from **Source 1** about the holiday in Turkey?   *(4 marks)*

The text gives lots of information about several activities and facilities suitable for young families. It would appeal to them because it is 'hassle-free', so parents can relax while their children enjoy themselves. Activities for young children include playing around the pool and going on a gentle boat trip. The hotel is near the harbour so it's not too far for small children to walk.

Here you will see that this student has recognised:
- the **purpose** of the text is to **inform**
- the **audience** is **parents with young families**.

This has helped her to pick out relevant information to use in her answer.

Source 1

A tour for toddlers

Exodus's Turkey Toddler Adventure has been designed with young families in mind. It's a hassle-free mix of relaxing and exploring, based in a harbour town in southern Turkey. Activities include a gentle boat ride to an island, snorkelling over a sunken city, and castle and farm visits. The hotel, which is 10 minutes' walk from the harbour, has a good restaurant and an excellent pool area.

EXAM SKILL

Recognising the **purpose** and **audience** of a text will help you comment on how and why the following things are effective:
- the writer's choice of information
- the use of presentation and language.

Use this skill to help you improve the quality of your writing.

Now try this

Show your awareness of purpose and audience as you answer this exam-style question.

1 (b) What do you learn from **Source 2** about the tour of the Hebrides?   *(4 marks)*

Remember to think about:
- the purpose of the text
- its audience.

Source 2

A Grand Tour of the Hebrides

Our grand tour takes in all the beauty and diversity of this very special environment. Two comfortable hotels ensure that this holiday is as relaxing as possible while offering great variety and a true journey of discovery which will live long in the memory.

Putting it into practice

In Section A, Question I (a) of your exam, you will need to retrieve information from a text. Read **Source** I, then look at the question on the next page.

Source 1

Two hours' homework a night linked to better school results

Spending more than two hours a night doing homework is linked to achieving better results in English, maths and science, according to a major study which has tracked the progress of 3,000 children over the past 15 years.

Spending any time doing homework showed benefits, but the effects were greater for students who put in two to three hours a night, according to the study published by the Department for Education.

The finding on homework runs counter to previous research which shows a 'relatively modest' link between homework and achievement at secondary school.

The academics involved in the latest research say their study emphasises what students actually do, rather than how much work the school has set.

Pam Sammons, a Professor of Education at Oxford University, said that time spent on homework reflected the influence of the school – whether students were expected to do homework – as well as students' enjoyment of their subjects.

Sammons said: 'That's one of the reasons Indian and Chinese students do better. They tend to put more time in. It's to do with your effort as well as your ability.

'What we're not saying is that everyone should do large amounts, but if we could shift some of those who spend no time or half an hour into [doing] one to two hours – one of the reasons private schools' results are better is that there's more expectation of homework.'

The research also finds that students who reported that they enjoyed school got better results. 'This is in contrast to findings during primary school where "enjoyment of school" was not related to academic attainment,' researchers said.

Schools could ensure children had a better experience by improving the 'behavioural climate', making schoolwork interesting and making children feel supported by teachers, Sammons said.

'Children who did well from disadvantaged backgrounds were backed by parents who valued learning and encouraged extra-curricular activities. 'Parents' own resilience in the face of hardship provided a role model for their children's efforts,' the research says.

The study underlines the importance of a good primary school. Children who attended an 'academically effective' primary school did better at maths and science in later life. The study did not find a link with performance in English.

Ministers have scrapped guidelines setting out how much homework children should be set amid criticism that it can interfere with family life. Scrapping the guidelines frees head teachers to set their own homework policy, the government says.

Putting it into practice

Look at this exam-style question and read the extracts from two sample student answers.

Retrieving information and ideas

For a question like this you should:

☑ spend about 5–6 minutes on your answer

☑ skim read the source first to get the main ideas

☑ read the source carefully and highlight **relevant information**

☑ check that the information you have highlighted is relevant.

Worked example

1 (a) Read **Source 1**. List **four** things that the study shows about homework and school.
    (4 marks)

Sample answer

Some people did a <u>study of more than 3,000 school</u> students. They said that <u>students who do more than two hours homework a night get better results.</u> This is different to another study, which said homework didn't make much difference.

✗ This point does not answer the question. It is also inaccurate: the research studied *around* 3,000 students.

✓ A sound point: accurate and relevant to the question.

✗ Another irrelevant point.

Improved sample answer

The study shows that <u>doing more than two hours homework a night helps students' achievement in English, maths and science.</u> <u>How much homework students actually do is more important than how much homework the school gives them</u> and <u>private schools get better results because they expect students to do more homework.</u>

✓ A relevant point.

✓ Two linked points

Now try this

The 'Improved sample answer' lists **three** things. How many more would this student need to add in order to achieve full marks?

Complete the 'Improved sample answer'.

Remember to:
• select only information relevant to the task
• do not copy out chunks of text: use your own words.

11

The writer's viewpoint

If you can identify a writer's viewpoint, you will be able to understand their ideas and write about them much more successfully.

Viewpoint

A **viewpoint** is the writer's attitude and opinion on a particular subject.

- Most texts reveal something about the writer's viewpoint.
- But in some texts the writer gives the facts as clearly as possible without revealing their own viewpoint. These texts are **unbiased**.

Identifying the writer's viewpoint

 Decide whether the viewpoint is positive or negative.

Source 1

Animal testing is the beauty industry's well-kept <u>ugly secret</u>

Many consumers still shop under the <u>assumption</u> that cosmetics animal suffering is a thing of the past. The truth, however, is altogether <u>harder to swallow</u>: thousands of animals are still used to test cosmetic chemicals.

 Look closely at these things to develop your understanding.

- **The heading:** suggests the writer thinks the beauty industry is covering up a horrible truth.
- **The writer's choice of ideas:** opening paragraph focuses on the difference between consumers' 'assumption' and 'the truth'.
- **The writer's choice of language:** immediate focus on 'animal suffering'.

Now try this

Read the next paragraph of the article. How does it tell you more about the writer's point of view?

Write **one** or **two** sentences commenting on the writer's:
- choice of ideas
- use of language.

Many companies continue to test on animals in countries such as the United States of America, China and Brazil. In these countries, animals continue to have cosmetic chemicals forced down their throats, dripped into their eyes and applied to their shaved skin, sometimes in doses high enough to kill.

Fact, opinion and expert evidence

Writers make their ideas more persuasive or convincing by supporting them with facts, opinions and expert evidence.

fact
Something that can be **proved** to be true.
Example: *'Manchester is a city in the United Kingdom.'*

opinion
An idea or viewpoint that the writer or speaker **believes** to be true.
Example: *'Manchester is the greatest city on earth.'*

expert evidence
Facts or opinions provided by an expert on the subject
Example: *'Barry Chesham, a travel writer with over 30 years' experience, says: 'Manchester is the greatest city on earth.'*

Improving your exam answer

Referring to how the writer has used facts, opinions and expert evidence can improve your answers.

Read **Source 1**. In this article, the writer has:
- made his viewpoint very clear by opening with **a strong opinion**
- supported his opinion with **a fact** – a statistic used as evidence to prove his point
- referred to **expert evidence** to support his point even more.

Source 1

Gang culture turning kids to lives of crime

A severe epidemic in Britain's inner cities has seen boys as young as eight are being coerced to join older street thugs

A 10.6 per cent increase in serious youth violence in the six months to last October has been linked to gangs. The Metropolitan Police's new anti-gang squad recently arrested 315 suspected gang members.

According to Scotland Yard, there are 250 gangs in London, each with several hundred members.

In Croydon, Surrey, one of the flashpoints of last summer's riots, I meet 13-year-old James.

'Three older boys said I should join their gang,' James remembers. 'They wanted me to look after things for them so they wouldn't get caught.'

'I was really afraid. I didn't think I would get away. I was surrounded, and I was followed a few times after that.'

He was lucky. David Mitchell, who runs the Gang Avoidance Project in Nottingham, says many school-age gang recruits are made to look after drugs and weapons with no firm promise of being accepted.

However, once they are involved, the financial rewards can be huge. 'They believe there is nothing else out there,' says Mr Mitchell. 'Some can easily make £4,000 a week.'

Now try this

Read **Source 1**. Note down **one** further fact, **one** further opinion and **one** further piece of expert evidence that the writer uses to support his viewpoint.

Make sure you know the difference between a fact, an opinion, and expert evidence.

Inference

A writer does not always state their meaning **explicitly**. Sometimes you have to **infer** what the writer is suggesting or **implying**.

Reading between the lines

When you read an extract, you can infer information about the **feelings**, **thoughts**, **attitudes** and **actions** of the writer and the people they are writing about.

Source 1

Six days to get up...
90 seconds to get down

Russian climber and BASE jumper Valery Rozov recently added another <u>highlight</u> to his incredible career in extreme sports by setting a <u>new world record</u> with a jump from the top of Shivling, a <u>6543m mountain</u> in the Indian part of the Himalayas.

Suggests a major achievement.

Suggests the writer's positive attitude to this achievement.

Implies this is an extraordinary feat.

Implies the extreme scale and danger of Rozov's jump.

Worked example

Read **Source 1**, then answer this exam-style question:

1 (b) What do you learn from **Source 1** about Valery Rozov?   *(4 marks)*

Rozov is a climber and base jumper who performs amazing stunts. The writer describes his career as 'incredible' and this jump as a 'highlight' suggesting it is one of his most extraordinary feats. The writer emphasises this by pointing out the height of the mountain and that Rozov set a new world record. This shows the scale and danger of the jump.

Using one-word quotations allows you to focus on the inferences made by the writer.

A fully developed answer should:
- refer to evidence from the extract
- comment on what can be inferred from the evidence
- develop the point with further comments or additional evidence from the source.

Now try this

Read the next paragraph of the newspaper article.

1 (b) What do you learn about Valery Rozov from this paragraph?   *(4 marks)*

Remember to choose quotations of just **one** or **two** words to support your answer, and comment on what each word implies.

The 47-year-old Russian's breathtaking feats, such as jumping into the active volcano Kamtschatka and from Ulvetanna Peak in the Antarctic, have made him famous the world over.

Thanks to his exceptional climbing skills, Rozov recently took things to the next level by completing the most challenging BASE jump ever performed.

Point-Evidence-Explain

P-E-E is a technique you can use in your answers to make them clearer and better organised.
- First, you make your **point**.
- Then you provide **evidence** to support it.
- Finally you should **explain** what the evidence tells us.

In Section A, Questions I (b), 2, 3 and 4, you will be asked to **write about**, **explain** or **compare** features of source texts. To do this effectively, you need to **support** your ideas with **evidence** from the text, and **explain** its **effect**.

P-E-E in practice

You should use a range of connecting phrases to link your point, evidence and explanation.

1 Make your point: The writer uses

The article focuses on

2 Introduce your evidence: For example,

The writer describes   For instance,

3 Introduce your explanation: This gives the impression that

The writer is implying that   This suggests   This shows

Worked example

Read **Source 1** opposite.

1 (b) What do you learn about the farmers' reactions to the problems they face?

(4 marks)

One reaction is that the farmers are going to demonstrate against the cut in milk prices. They are doing this 'to make their feelings known'. This suggests that they have reacted with strong feelings to these cuts.

Source 1

The cut in supermarket milk prices is crippling dairy farmers, who are now planning to take part in demonstrations to make their feelings known. They say that the price cut is causing major financial problems for farmers and their employees.

The paragraph opens with a clear **point**, focusing on the farmers' reactions.

The point is supported with **evidence**: a short quotation from the article.

An **explanation** shows how the evidence answers the question.

Now try this

1 Read the extract opposite. Choose a short quotation to support the following point:

> The writer uses a stream of negative language to describe Britain.

2 Now write a sentence commenting on the writer's choice of language.

Remember to use connecting phrases to link your **point**, **evidence** and **explanation**.

Switzerland: the sort of country Britain should try to be

Compared to sleazy, crime-ridden Britain, with its stagnant economy, soaring unemployment, decaying social services, mushrooming debts and uncontrolled state spending – not to mention its useless, clueless and incompetent political leadership – Switzerland is still what Britain once was: an island of the blessed, a patch of prosperity in a continent sliding into a black hole.

15

Putting it into practice

In Section A, Question I of your exam, you will need to locate and retrieve information and ideas from a text. Read **Source 1** then look at the question on the next page.

Source 1

Scott Mills: my Saturday job

The Radio 1 DJ explains how volunteering, passion and persistence led to his dream career

I was 12 when I started working at a local hospital radio station in Southampton, near where I grew up. I'd always wanted to do radio from as far back as I can remember. Actually, I think I got the job because my nan rang them up! I spent two years volunteering – on a Tuesday evening and all day on Saturday.

Initially I just helped out behind the scenes – in the newsroom, making tea, being the general dogsbody. I was nervous because I was quite shy. I wasn't the best at meeting new people, but I got better at it and grew in confidence.

Some people there were more welcoming than others, but despite my age I think it was clear that I really wanted to do this as a career. The committee were all in their 60s and a bit old-school. They had been doing the hospital radio in the same way forever; I think some of them are still there now. When a 12-year-old comes along and is very keen they are a bit ... oh, who is this? Eventually they chucked me out for being too young.

There was a younger crowd in on Sundays, who were in their 20s and who I could relate to. So I went in on Sundays and they let me do loads: operating equipment and going on air. The first thing I would do on air was the chart rundown, which I prepared lovingly every week.

I remember when my friend Lee, who I'm still in contact with, sat me down one day and said: 'Right, let's see how good you are.' So we did an off-air radio show where I operated all of the equipment. I remember being the most excited I've ever been. But eventually the older people sent me a letter saying I couldn't operate the

equipment because I was too young – they basically told me not to come in any more. I think it was something to do with not being insured. I was gutted. I used to love it.

I never thought I'd make it as a presenter because I wasn't confident enough. I was planning on working behind the scenes, not as a presenter. This was the first time I realised I could do it. Before that, it was just a dream.

I'm from a small town in Hampshire; I had a dream of what I wanted to do and I followed it through. If I hadn't hung out with those hospital radio people on a voluntary basis, I wouldn't have had the skills to get my first job.

Putting it into practice

Look at the exam-style question below and read the extracts from two students' answers.

Worked example

1 (b) Read **Source 1**. What do you learn from Scott Mills' article about the Radio 1 DJ's early life?   *(4 marks)*

Sample answer

Scott Mills was shy when he was young so he thought he would not make it as a presenter and end up working behind the scenes, and not be a presenter although he dreamed of it and loved it when he tried it. Hospital radio was where he got the skills to get his first job.

Retrieving information and ideas

For a question like this you should:
- ☑ spend about 6 minutes
- ☑ skim-read the source first to get the main ideas
- ☑ read the source carefully and highlight **relevant information**
- ☑ check that the information you have highlighted is relevant.

✓ Clear points focused on answering the question.

✗ The points are not supported with evidence or fully explained.

✗ This information is copied almost word for word from the source.

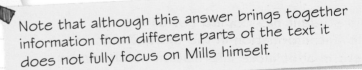

Note that although this answer brings together information from different parts of the text it does not fully focus on Mills himself.

Improved sample answer

Scott Mills was 12 when he went to work in local hospital radio. He spent two years there 'volunteering' until he was 'chucked out' because he was too young. This shows that he was dedicated because he worked for nothing and was ambitious from an early age.

✓ Selects key information.

✓ Supported with evidence.

✓ Explains what this suggests about Mills' early life.

Now try this

Complete the 'Improved sample answer', aiming to identify at least **three** more relevant points.

Remember to:
- select relevant information from the whole text
- support your points with evidence and explanation
- avoid copying relevant information word for word.

17

Selecting evidence

It is important to always support your answers with carefully chosen, relevant evidence from the text.

Relevant evidence

The evidence you choose must support your points **and** allow you to comment closely on the writer's choices. To do this, you should choose evidence that:

- will help you answer the question
- contains a word, phrase or sentence structure that will help you to explain the effect.

Worked example

1 (b) Read **Source 1**. What do you learn about the sport of free running? *(4 marks)*

Sample answer

Free running is when you hurl yourself around a city 'using ledges, handrails and anything else within reach' to do backflips and somersaults.

This student has copied out all the relevant information in the extract but there is a lot more information which can be **inferred** from the writer's use of language.

Remember to:
- show your understanding by explaining in your own words
- support your ideas using the text.

Source 1

Free runners hit the streets as urban craze sweeps Britain

It is one of the hottest days of the summer and outside London's South Bank Centre Jake Penny (15) and his friend, Joe Scandrett (13), are hurling themselves around a warren of concrete pedestrian underpasses. Using ledges, metal handrails and anything else within reach, the two teenagers cause passers-by to gape by executing back-flips and somersaults high into the air; each time landing gracefully and silently on the pavement. What is the appeal of this peculiar sport in the urban jungle?

Improved sample answer

'hurling themselves' suggests danger, recklessness, action ...

'gape' suggests spectators and writer are amazed and impressed ...

'gracefully and silently' suggests impressed with their skill ...

'What is the appeal of this peculiar sport in the urban jungle?' is a rhetorical question that suggests the writer doesn't understand its appeal ... Perhaps it is a sport for younger people?

These quotations provide lots of opportunities for effective explanations that will help you to improve your response.

Now try this

Write **two** or **three** P-E-E paragraphs answering the exam-style question above.

 Remember to choose quotations that will help you to **answer the question**. (You can use the examples given, or choose some of your own.)

Embedding quotations

You can use long quotes or short quotes as evidence.

Longer quotations

When you use a longer quotation you should give it some space.

Sample answer

The writer uses a rhetorical question to sum up the key point in her article: 'Why do some people feel they can say things on a social networking website which they would not dare to say to someone's face?' This question engages the reader, making them consider this key point, and also suggests that she is horrified and mystified by the way people behave on the internet.

Longer quotes: what to do

1 Introduce your longer quotation with a colon.

2 Start the quotation on a new line.

3 Put your quotation in quotation marks.

4 Copy your quotation accurately.

5 Start your explanation on a new line.

Shorter quotations

When you use shorter quotations you should aim to embed them in your paragraph.

Sample answer

The writer condemns some users of social networking websites as 'cruel' and 'offensive' although she does confess that she has become 'obsessed' with them. This strong choice of positive and negative language suggests that she has mixed feelings about these sites.

Short quotes: what to do

Remember these things.

1 You do not need to introduce each quotation with a colon or start a new line.

2 Put each quotation in quotation marks.

3 Make sure the sentence containing the embedded quotations makes sense.

4 Choose single-word quotations very carefully to ensure you can make an effective comment on them.

The effect of short quotes

Shorter quotations are often more effective than longer ones.

- They show that you can identify key words and phrases in the text.
- They allow you to focus on the writer's specific language choices.
- You don't waste time and ink copying out large chunks of the source text.

Source 1

Why sport matters

Stars at the Olympics, like those at Wimbledon, can **inspire** young people to develop their own talents and build their own **self-respect**, whether they are brilliant or just run-of-the-mill at the games they learn to love. Team sports help bind people and communities together. **Sport brings young people out of themselves, away from computer and television screens**. It makes them **healthy** and **motivated**.

Now try this

Read **Source 1** then write **two** P-E-E paragraphs explaining what you learn about the benefits of sport from the article. Use the bold quotations to help you.

 You could use the longer quotation in one paragraph, and **all** the shorter quotations in the other.

Develop your explanations

It is important to select relevant points and effective evidence, but your explanations are where you answer the question and show how strong your reading skills are. You should aim to give an effective and developed explanation for each of your points and evidence.

Worked example

2   Read **Source 1**. Bear Grylls is an adventurer and television presenter. What do you learn about him from this extract?

Remember to:
  • show your understanding by explaining in your own words
  • support your ideas using the text.

(8 marks)

Sample answer

At the start of the extract, Grylls seems confident. He describes the jump he is about to make as 'Steep but manageable'. The word 'steep' suggests he knows that it is dangerous, and the word 'manageable' makes him sound quite arrogant. The short sentence adds to this. It sounds like he is not worried about the danger.

Notice how this explanation makes three very specific comments.
  • Two of them focus on individual language choices, explaining their effect and how they influence the reader's perception of the writer.
  • The third comments on the effect of the writer's choice of sentence structure.

Source 1

Mud, sweat and tears

'You set, buddy?' cameraman Simon asks me, smiling. His rig is all prepped and ready.

Beneath me is three hundred feet of steep snow and ice. Steep but manageable.

I leap.

I am soon traveling at over 40mph. Feet first down the mountain. The ice races past only inches from my head. This is my world.

I gain even more speed. The edge of the peak gets closer. Time to arrest the fall.

I flip nimbly onto my front and drive the ice axe into the snow. A cloud of white spray and ice soars into the air. It works like it always does. Like clockwork. Total confidence. I am now static.

The world hangs still. Then – bang.

Simon, his heavy wooden sled, plus solid metal camera housing, pile straight into my left thigh. He is doing in excess of 45mph.

There is an instant explosion of pain and noise and white.

It is like a freight train. And I am thrown down the mountain like a doll.

Now try this

Look again at **Source 1**. Write at least **one** further P-E-E paragraph which answers the exam-style question above.

  • Remember to use linking phrases to connect your point evidence and explanation.
  • Aim to develop your explanation, commenting on **one or two** features of your chosen quotation.

Word classes

To help you comment on a writer's choice of language, think about the types of words they use.

Nouns

These are words used to describe:
- objects: e.g. table, building, dog, tree
- people: e.g. man, grandma, Ryan, mechanic
- places: e.g. town, countryside, London
- ideas: e.g. happiness, prejudice, religion.

Verbs

These are words used to describe:
- actions: e.g. to kick, to run, to fly
- occurrences: e.g. to fall, to collapse, to happen
- states: e.g. to be, to think, to wonder.

Remember: **pronouns** replace or stand in for nouns – e.g. I, you, he, our, theirs.

Remember: **adverbs** describe verbs – e.g. suddenly, quickly, luckily, often, usually, sometimes. They are usually (**but not always**) formed by adding -ly to an adjective.

Adjectives

These are words to describe a noun: e.g. good, red, large, nice, famous.

Remember: **adjectives** can become **comparatives** (e.g. better, larger) and **superlatives** (e.g. best, largest).

Comparatives and superlatives

Make sure you are familiar with these and how to use them.

Comparatives give degrees of difference: e.g. better, redder, nicer, more famous.

Superlatives give the most or least: e.g. best, reddest, nicest, most famous.

Examples

Here are some comments about the extracts opposite, focusing on word class:

1 He crouches, springs, and flies, eventually crashing to the ground in a cloud of dust.

The writer uses a stream of action verbs to create a sense of urgent and dramatic movement.

2 I run into the trees, panting. I look round. There is no one else here. It is dark. I am alone.

The writer focuses the reader on the pace of the action by using very few descriptive adverbs or adjectives.

3 The snow drifts delicately on a gentle breeze, swirling slowly.

The writer paints a vivid picture with a rich choice of adjectives and adverbs.

Now try this

Write **one** sentence about **each** of these two extracts, focusing on word class and its effect.

The table groans with glistening green apples, hefty bowlfuls of muddy brown potatoes, and fluorescent red cherries.

Children come running, screaming, shouting, bawling and falling towards me.

Putting it into practice

In Section A, Question 2 of your exam, you must demonstrate that you can understand and infer meaning in a text. Read **Source 1** then look at the question on the next page.

Source 1

I couldn't read until I was 60

By Sue Chapman

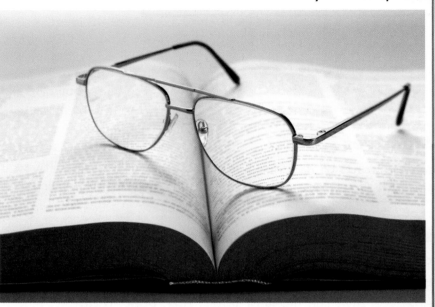

The moment I realised *A* was for *apple* was incredible. Such a simple thing; such a life-changing moment. I was a pensioner, a grandma, and had spent a lifetime keeping the terrible secret that I couldn't read or write.

For the whole of my adult years, I'd lived a half-life, never daring to socialise, apply for jobs or even try new recipes for fear of being discovered. Ever since my schooldays, when the teacher used to stick pins in me during sewing class for not being able to follow the instructions, I have been filled with shame and embarrassment.

As a child, I can remember being totally baffled. The teachers quickly classed me as stupid and lazy, and I switched off. I became adept at hiding the fact that I hadn't learned to read. I watched the other children enjoying their books in the library and copied them, even laughing occasionally to be more convincing. I didn't realise turning the pages from right to left was wrong, though.

I was terribly bullied by both children and teachers, and had no friends. My parents didn't care about my problems in class, and I became so used to being called stupid that I came to believe it was true. My self-esteem was at rock bottom and I left school at 15, unable even to recognise the alphabet.

My husband remained unaware of my inability to read for the whole of our marriage. I organised it so he did all the paperwork and I did the housework – I was sure he'd leave me if he found out the truth. My two boys, Kevin and David, came along and I felt awful that I couldn't help as they started to learn to read themselves. But as I never read to them from the start, it wasn't something they questioned.

The turning point came at 60, during a bout of depression. A volunteer from a local charity came to read to me, for company. When she suggested we read to each other, I refused, but she was so persistent, in such a warm way, that I finally confessed I didn't know how. She arranged adult learning classes but I was so petrified, it took me three laps of the car park before I went in.

After six months I could write a sentence. A year later I won an adult learners award and spent the £200 prize money on a Kindle. Finally I can read all those books I'd wondered about. My goal is to take my GCSEs.

Putting it into practice

Look at the exam-style question below and read the two sample student answers.

Worked example

2 What problems did Sue Chapman face because she could not read or write?

Remember to:
- show your understanding by explaining in your own words
- support your ideas using the text.

(8 marks)

Understanding and inferring meaning

For a question like this you should:

☑ spend about 12 minutes

☑ read the source carefully and highlight relevant words, phrases and sentences

☑ support all your points with evidence and a clear explanation of how your evidence answers the question.

Sample answer

The writer says it was incredible when she learnt to read. It was a problem she had for her whole life.

It stopped her doing lots of things she wanted to do like socialising, applying for jobs or even trying new recipes.

It also meant that the teachers at school thought she was stupid.

✗ This point is not fully relevant: it does not focus on the problems the writer faced.

✗ These are both valid points but are not supported with evidence or explanation.

Improved sample answer

The biggest problem that Sue Chapman faced was having to hide her secret that she could not read or write. She explains all the things she could not do for fear of being discovered such as 'socialise' and 'apply for jobs' because she was 'filled with shame and embarrassment'. This suggests it has made her whole life very difficult.

✓ An effective point summing up the writer's problems.

✓ Embedded quotations showing the problems and their consequences.

An effective explanation showing understanding of the impact of the writer's problems.

Now try this

Complete the 'Improved sample answer', aiming to identify at least **two** more relevant points.

Remember to:
- check that all your points focus on the writer's thoughts and feelings
- support all your points with carefully chosen quotations and detailed explanations.

Connotations

Some words can create bigger ideas in our minds through the ideas and attitudes they suggest. These ideas and attitudes are called **connotations**.

Thinking about what a word or phrase suggests can help you to write effective comments on the writer's choice of language.

Look at what the word 'squeaked' could suggest in the example opposite.

> 'Help!' I <u>squeaked</u>.

The connotation of the word 'squeaked' suggests the narrator or writer is like a mouse. This, in turn, suggests they might be small, timid and frightened.

Language choice

These sentences have similar literal meanings. But the connotations let you know the writer's **real attitude**.

1 An unfamiliar aroma wafts through the air.

2 A strange smell fills the air.

3 A weird stench seeps through the air.

> If you explore the connotations of a writer's language choice, it can help you write about their attitude.

Source 1

Freak shows

Our TV screens are filled nightly with otherwise obscure people who suffer <u>gross</u> physical deformities. The justification for <u>exposing</u> them is that making public the difficulties of such lives is a healthy, cathartic process. But are the producers' motives any better than those who ran <u>freak shows</u> in Victorian times, as depicted in *The Elephant Man*? The TV shows pull in a <u>lowing herd</u> of undiscerning viewers who, in turn, attract advertising from firms which prosper by targeting them.

Read **Source I** opposite. The writer conveys his viewpoint through the connotations of the language he has chosen.

This literally means **large** or **extreme**, but also carries connotations of revulsion.

This literally means **showing** or **revealing**, but also has connotations suggesting being made vulnerable, perhaps to ridicule or embarrassment.

This refers to people with deformities who were put on display for misguided visitors' entertainment. It has strong connotations of exploitation.

Now try this

Look again at **Source 1**.

1 Write a sentence commenting on what the writer is suggesting by describing the viewers of these programmes as a 'lowing herd'.

2 Write another sentence explaining what this suggests about the writer's attitude to viewers of these television programmes.

Rhetorical devices 1

You will need to think about the range of language or rhetorical devices that writers use to emphasise their point or manipulate the reader's response.

Comment on rhetorical devices

Don't just name the rhetorical devices. Remember to explain the effect they have.

You can make very **effective comments** on language by thinking about the effect of rhetorical devices.

Here are some examples.

Alliteration: two or more words close to each other that begin with the same sound. Can be used to emphasise an idea.

The writer uses alliteration in the title, emphasising the key point of the text.

Rhetorical question: a question used to engage the reader.
Hint: Look for question marks in the text.

Opening the article with a rhetorical question immediately engages the reader, encouraging them to ask themselves the question and keep reading to discover the answer.

Pattern of three: a rhythmic trio of words or phrases used for emphasis.
Synonym: a word or phrase that means the same as another word or phrase.

The writer uses a pattern of three synonyms to highlight how busy London is.

Repetition: a repeated word or phrase to emphasise an idea.

Repetition emphasises how different London is to the rest of the country.

Lists: a series of items or ideas, often used to highlight quantity or variety.

The writer draws our attention to the pace and variety of life in London with a long list.

Source 1

London welcomes the world

Why is our capital so busy, active and bustling? The same cannot be said of the nation as a whole. But London is different. London is a competitive Babel of commercial interests, immigrant populations, national politics, artistic energy, media, administration, monarchy, students and tourists. Because of the English language and its large (though poorly run) airports, it is a hub for half the globe. It is hard to think of anything you could not buy there or anyone you could not meet. More than of any other city today, you can say of London that if you have not been there, you have not really seen the world.

Whatever the fluctuating fortunes of the rest of Britain, the activity never stops. People who live in London get cynical about all the praise heaped on its 'buzz' and 'vibrancy'. These can be codewords for drugs, late-night noise and multi-culturalism run riot. It may be difficult that so many citizens of the world seek refuge, or fame, or fortune, in our grimy capital, but it is, broadly speaking, a compliment that they do so. Better to welcome the world than to hide from it.

Now try this

Look at the second paragraph in **Source 1**. Identify **two** more examples of rhetorical devices. Write **one** or **two** sentences about the effect each one is intended to have on the reader.

Remember, an answer that **comments on the effect** of a rhetorical device is better than one that only names the device.

Rhetorical devices 2

You will need to think about the range of language or rhetorical devices that writers use to emphasise their point or manipulate the reader's response.

Comment on rhetorical devices

You can make very effective comments on language by thinking about the effect of rhetorical devices.
Here are some examples.

> Don't just name the rhetorical devices. Remember to explain the effect they have.

Emotive language: words intended to create an extreme response or play on the reader's emotions.

The writer uses emotive language to suggest that young people are terrified by their fear of failure.

Hyperbole: exaggeration used to make a point.

The writer uses hyperbole to emphasise young people's expectations, suggesting that they are totally unrealistic.

Contrast: comparing two opposing or different ideas to emphasise the difference between them.

The writer repeatedly contrasts today's young people with other groups to make her point.

A short sentence: a short punchy sentence used to emphasise a dramatic point.

The writer finishes on a short sentence, summarising her point in a hard-hitting and dramatic conclusion.

Source 2

Why so many children are failing to grow up

Throughout school, I worked every Saturday and every holiday. My generation was obsessed with work: we wanted to earn money, to have good careers, to make something of our lives. And we were prepared to start at the bottom to do so.

Our children, by contrast, have a sense of entitlement coupled with a paralysing fear of failure. It starts with the pressure we put them under to succeed academically: in consequence, many of them work hard at school and strive to get into good universities.

But having achieved the academic success that was demanded of them, they are bemused not to be offered the world on a plate.

In countries where it's still considered normal to strive, you won't hear it much discussed. Chinese and Indian children are in no doubt about why they're working so hard at school: in order to enter careers that enable them not only to raise their own families but to take care of their parents, too.

Our children, by contrast, have been raised in an infantilising culture that tells them nothing should be unfair or hard or uncomfortable. Of course some of them haven't grown up. They haven't been taught how to.

Now try this

Look at **Source 2**. Identify as many other examples of rhetorical device as you can. Write **one** or **two** sentences about the effect each one is intended to have on the reader.

EXAM SKILL

Make sure you are familiar with these devices:
• alliteration   • rhetorical question
• pattern of three   • list   • repetition   • contrast
• hyperbole   • emotive language   • short sentences

Use this skill to help you improve the quality of your writing.

Figurative language

You will need to remember that figurative language (also known as **imagery**) is used to create an image in the reader's mind.

Comment on figurative language

To improve your exam responses you will need to **comment on** the effect of figurative language in a text.

> Don't just name examples of figurative language. Remember to explain their **effect**.

Here are some examples.

Simile: a comparison, usually using 'as' or 'like', suggesting a resemblance between one thing and another – e.g. Her bedroom was like a prison.

The writer uses a simile to compare the size of the icebergs to the size of the ship. This not only gives the reader a sense of how huge they are but also makes them more threatening by suggesting they could overpower the ship in some way.

Metaphor: a direct comparison suggesting a resemblance between one thing and another – e.g. Her bedroom was a prison.

The writer uses a metaphor comparing the icebergs to jewels. This suggests that they are rare, precious, valuable and beautiful.

Personification: describing something non-human as if it were human – e.g. The leaves danced in the breeze.

The writer personifies the icebergs as placid giants suggesting their size but also hinting at the danger which they threaten.

Source 1

The white jewels of the Atlantic

WE WERE on a summer cruise along the Greenland coast, nudging our way past lumps of floating ice ranging from 'growlers' the size of a car to bergs almost as large as ships. It was the white jewels of ice floating serenely past the ship that most commanded our attention. Some, like vast uncut diamonds, were almost transparent.

It seemed a simple proposition to pull up alongside, leap across and explore these placid giants. They looked stable enough. Then a berg the size of our boat rolled completely over. The resultant waves made us hold on to the boat's rail and we saw why our skipper had exercised great caution in his navigation through the ice.

Eventually, as a floating white blanket of ice blocked our course, the engine was cut and a profound silence descended. Then an ice fragment was scooped from the water and a crew member began to smash it with a hammer. The ice sparkled in our glasses as we raised them in a toast to the crew and their boat, to the Greenlanders and their vast and beautiful land.

Now try this

Look at **Source 1**. Identify at least **two** more examples of figurative language. Write **one** or **two** sentences about the effect each example is intended to have on the reader.

> Remember: an answer that **comments on the effect** of figurative language will gain more marks than one which simply says 'it's a simile'.

Putting it into practice

In Section A, Question 3 of your exam, you will need to write about the ways language is used in texts. Read **Source 1** then look at the question on the next page.

Source 1

Cruise the Nile

Enjoy a cruise on the legendary River Nile and experience many of Egypt's ancient wonders along the way.

Great savings on Nile cruises

Accompanied by an Egyptologist, you will enjoy ten escorted excursions on board the five-star *Viking Princess*. The itinerary takes you from Luxor to Aswan, visiting spectacular ancient sites including the stunning Valley of the Kings, the burial place of the Pharaohs, and the breath-taking temples of Karnak and Luxor.

In Aswan you will see the Unfinished Obelisk and the Old Granite Quarries plus the Temple of Philae, famously featured in Agatha Christie's *Death on the Nile*.

SPECIAL OFFER – SAVE UP TO £200 PER PERSON

You can extend your holiday for a second week at historic Luxor from £139, or the Red Sea resort of El Gouna from £189. Alternatively combine the bustling city of Cairo with a stay in Luxor from £499.

Get up to £200 off per person on selected dates

In Cairo marvel at the amazing Pyramids and Great Sphinx or see the treasures of the boy king Tutankhamun in the Egyptian museum.

In Luxor enjoy a relaxing few days or explore more sights before returning home.

Putting it into practice

Look at this exam-style question and read the two sample student answers.

Worked example

3 How does the writer use **language features** to **inform** the reader and **persuade** the reader to book the holiday?

Remember to:
- give some examples of language features that inform
- give some examples of language features that persuade
- explain the effects.   *(12 marks)*

Writing about language

For a question like this you should:
- ☑ spend about 18 minutes
- ☑ read the source carefully and note effective use of language
- ☑ support all your points with evidence and a clear explanation focusing on **effect**.

Sample answer

The writer uses lots of language to persuade: 'Experience many of Egypt's ancient wonders.' This makes you want to go on the cruise and see these wonders. There are lots of details about the different things you can see which also makes you want to go and see them.

✗ A vague point that does not help to answer the question.

✗ Evidence given but no real explanation given of its effect.

This sentence is unsupported by evidence or detailed explanation.

Improved sample answer

The writer uses lots of positive language to persuade the reader to book the holiday. You can 'experience many of Egypt's ancient wonders'. The writer uses a command, almost telling you to book the holiday and describing what you will see as 'wonders' suggests the reader will be amazed at what they see.

Note how this point uses keywords from the question to ensure answering it.

✓ Supported with embedded evidence.

✓ A detailed comment on a language feature and its effect.

✓ A second detailed comment on language choice and its effect.

Now try this

Complete the 'Improved sample answer', aiming to identify at least **two** more relevant points.

Remember to focus on specific language choices and explain their effect.

Identifying sentence types

Make sure you can recognise the four basic types of sentence: simple, complex, compound and minor.

Simple sentences

These contain a subject and **one verb**. So they give **one piece of information** about an event or action. For example:

This is the verb.

> The dog <u>chased</u> the ball.

Compound sentences

These are a series of simple sentences joined together. So they contain **two or more verbs** and give **two or more pieces** of information about events or actions. For example:

These are the verbs.

> The dog <u>chased</u> the ball and <u>brought</u> it back.

Note how the pieces of information are joined with words such as **and**, **but** and **then**. In this example, the connecting word is **and**.

Minor sentences

These are grammatically incomplete because they do not contain a verb. For example:

> Poor dog.   Yes.   So what?

Complex sentences

These are longer sentences with one part dependent on another. So they contain **two or more verbs** and give **two or more pieces of information**. The piece that is most important is called the **main clause**. The other piece is called the **subordinating** or **dependent** clause, because it needs the main clause to make sense. For example:

This is the main clause.

> The dog chased the ball until <u>it was exhausted</u>.

This is the subordinating clause.

Note how the two clauses are joined with connecting words such as **because**, **although** and **if**. In this example, the connecting word is **until**.

Sometimes, the two clauses in a complex sentence can be swapped round. For example:

> Until it was exhausted, the dog chased the ball.

Now try this

What kind of sentences are these? How do you know?
1 Because he fell over, the child burst into tears.
2 He cried and cried.
3 He howled like a wolf.
4 When he finally stopped, his father smiled.
5 The father put the child to bed and listened carefully at his bedroom door.
6 Silence.

Commenting on sentence types

You will need to remember that **how** writers structure a sentence can have just as much impact on the reader as the **language** they choose.

Sentences and audience

Different sentence types can reflect a text's target reader. Look at these examples.

 A text aimed at younger children will use more (and sometimes nothing but) short simple sentences:

> Sally wants to play catch. She goes in the garden. The sun is shining.

 A complex text aimed at adults will use a variety of sentence types including longer, complex sentences:

> While European unity may be desirable for many politicians, it does not always appeal to members of the voting public who may feel that it represents a loss of nationhood and of independence.

Sentence and mood

Sentences can reflect the mood the writer is trying to create. Look at these examples.

 A longer complex sentence can suggest time dragging:

> We sat and we waited, watching the clock, tapping our toes, drumming our fingers anxiously on our knees, then pacing the floor until finally it was our turn.

 A series of shorter sentences can suggest anxiety and build tension:

> I stopped. I listened. I heard nothing.

Long and short sentences

Short, simple sentences can be used for dramatic effect. This can be accentuated when the short simple sentence follows a longer sentence. Look at these examples.

 Running through the woods, I darted between the trees, one eye always over my shoulder, the other peering into the distant darkness, scouring the shadows. Then I saw him.

Notice how the final short sentence provides a sudden and dramatic conclusion to the tension-building of the longer sentence.

 Many people are under the impression that GCSEs have become so easy that success is simply a matter of turning up, with or without a pen. They are wrong.

Notice how the final short sentence sharply dismisses the argument presented in the longer sentence.

Now try this

Choose any source text from any page of this guide. Find **three** sentences that the writer of that text has structured for effect. Write **one** or **two** sentences about the effect of each one.

Remember to look out for unusual sentence construction: short or long sentences, or a text consisting mainly of one type of sentence. Think: why has the writer done this? What effect is intended?

Making the best comments

The quality of your comments on a writer's choices can make the difference between an average answer and a really good one.

Read this exam question and **Source 1**.

> **3** How does the writer use **language features** to **describe** herself?
>
> Remember to:
> - give some examples of language features to describe
> - explain the effects. *(12 marks)*

Source 1

As a teenager I was horribly thin, had a mouth full of big frilly teeth, wore unflattering National Health glasses and was cursed with drab, beige hair that refused to curl, no matter what my mother did to it.

That was the external packaging – but inside, I was 100 per cent rebel. Mother Nature might have given me unpromising raw material, but I realised at 12 that my brain – not the curl of my hair – was my ultimate weapon.

 You could start your answer with a point and some evidence:

The writer describes herself from the beginning of the article. She tells the reader that when she was younger she was 'horribly thin' and 'cursed with drab, beige hair'.

Now you need to **explain** how the writer uses language to describe herself.

 Now you need to offer some explanations. You can do this by commenting on:

- **viewpoint**

  The writer gives the reader lots of description of her appearance before she goes on to say how unimportant it really is.

- **language choice**

  The word 'cursed' suggests this was one of the worst things that could possibly happen to her.

- **effect on the reader**

  The description engages the reader immediately and makes us feel sorry for the writer.

- **purpose**

  This description gives the reader a vivid picture of the writer, creating the impression that there is nothing she liked about her appearance.

- **sentence structure**

  This long sentence lists lots of negative features showing how disappointed the writer was with her appearance.

  Remember, you can make comments on any combination of these things.

Now try this

Write a second point about **Source 1**. Support it with evidence from the text. Then write **at least two** different **explanations** commenting on **either** viewpoint **or** purpose **or** language choice **or** sentence structure **or** the effect on the reader.

Comment on language and purpose: argue and persuade

In Section A, Question 3, you could be asked to write about how the writer has used language to **argue**, **persuade** or **advise**.

Argument and persuasive texts

These texts use a range of language features to **influence** the reader's **opinions** and **actions**. For example:

- newspaper articles express a writer's opinion, trying to convince the reader to agree
- advertisements try to persuade the reader to buy a product or service
- charity appeals try to persuade the reader to support their cause
- an advice leaflet suggests ways in which the reader can solve or deal with a problem.

How writers do it

Writers argue and persuade by using rhetorical devices such as:

- rhetorical questions
- emotive language
- direct access
- lists
- repetition
- contrast.

 Rhetorical questions persuade by leading readers to an obvious answer supporting their argument:

> Would you like to make a lot of money for doing almost nothing?

 Emotive language influences the reader's view of a particular idea or situation:

> A **crisis** sounds much more serious than a **problem**.

 Direct address is when the writer talks directly to the reader. It involves the reader and encourages them to act:

> You can make a difference with a donation of just 50p a month.

 Contrast emphasises the negative or positive elements in an argument:

> You have everything.
>
> He has nothing.

 Notice how a contrast like this could persuade you to help someone more disadvantaged than you.

 Lists are used to demonstrate the range or appeal of ideas in an argument. For example, this list emphasises just how useful this product is for everyone:

> This product is great for men, women, children, and even pets!

 Repeating a word or phrase effectively hammers home the point the writer wants to make. For example:

> Of all the mad ideas in our mad world, this is the maddest.

Now try this

Choose **two** source texts from this guide that argue or persuade. How many **rhetorical devices** can you identify in them? Write a sentence commenting on the effect of each one.

Comment on language and purpose: describe

In Section A, Question 3, you could be asked to write about how the writer has used language to describe.

Descriptive texts

Descriptive texts use a range of features to **create a picture** in the reader's mind. For example:
- travel writing – describes a place or a journey
- autobiographical writing – describes an event or experience.

How writers do it

Writers describe by using:
- language choice
- figurative language
- the five senses
- feelings

The five senses covers descriptions of:

> sight, sound, smell, touch and taste.

Remember that you can comment on **either** individual examples of sensory description **or** the quantity of sensory description the writer uses in the text.

1 **Language choice**

In a piece of description, the writer will have chosen their language very carefully, thinking hard about connotation and its impact on the reader.

> I perched precariously on my sledge as we hurtled across the frozen wasteland.

> I sat on my sledge as we went over the ice.

Look out for opportunities to comment on descriptive language. For example, in the first sentence the writer suggests danger (**perched**), speed (**hurtled**) and a hostile environment (**wasteland**).

3 **Figurative language** creates a picture in the reader's mind through the use of imagery or figurative language.
For example:
- similes
- metaphor
- personification.

Remember to comment on the effect of the figurative language and what it suggests to the reader.

4 **Feelings** are often described using their physical effect on the writer. This helps recreate these feelings in the reader. For example:

> My heart thumped and my mouth went dry. I was terrified.

Remember that a writer is trying to create tension for the reader, so they will read on to see what happened.

Now try this

Look at **Source 1** on page 25 and **Source 1** on page 32. How many **key descriptive features** can you identify in them? Write a sentence commenting on the effect of each one.

Comment on language and purpose: inform and explain

In Section A, Question 3, you could be asked to write about how the writer has used language to **inform** and **explain**.

Information and explanation texts

Information texts include:
- encyclopedia entries
- fact sheets
- reports.

They aim to present the reader with facts.

Explanation texts include:
- instruction manuals
- school textbooks
- any text that answers the questions 'How?' and 'Why?'.

How writers do it

Information and explanation texts do not use as many language features as persuasive or descriptive texts. Instead, writers use other features such as:
- structure
- tone
- facts
- statistics.

> Get used to looking out for and commenting on the effect of these features.

 1 Structure

Information and explanation texts **do** follow a logical structure, often in chronological order. To signpost this to the reader, they sometimes use connectives such as:
- First, ...
- Then ...
- Next ...
- Finally, ...

2 Tone

Some explanation and information texts use informal language to appeal to their intended audience, e.g. a leaflet aimed at teenagers may use more abbreviations and slang. More often, they have a formal tone or register. To achieve this, they use:
- formal language
- standard English
- the third person (he, she, they).

> Note that these suggest the information is impartial, unbiased, accurate and reliable.

 3 Facts and statistics

Information and explanation texts often use a range of facts and statistics to achieve their purpose. They highlight key facts like this:

> In the last year, nearly 2,000 people have been killed on Britain's roads.

Facts and statistics convey to the reader that the text, and the information or explanation it gives, can be trusted and relied upon.

Now try this

Look at **Source 1** on page 36 and **Source 2** on page 46. How many of the **key features on this page** can you identify in them? Write a sentence commenting on the effect of each one.

Putting it into practice

In Section A, Question 3 of your exam, you will need to write about the ways language is used in texts. Read **Source I** then look at the question on the next page.

Source 1

Probably the best beach in the world: a real slice of paradise in the beautiful Bahamas

There are beaches – and there are BEACHES.

Harbour Island's eastern shore on the Atlantic coast has been blessed by the Gods of Tourism with a long deep beach that runs without interruption for three miles along the entire length of the island.

The locals call it North Beach but it is also known as Pink Sands, and here's what makes it a world beater: it's not your conventional sticky yellow sand, it's a pinkish sand that is incredibly fine, more like icing sugar and as soft as an eiderdown to walk or lie on.

There's virtually no seaweed in or out of the water (I hate seaweed … really hate it). There is a total absence of cigarette butts, old beer bottles, cans, bits of Elastoplast, used tissues or other charming flotsam so often deposited on so many waterfronts.

There are no pebbles, sharp stones, rocks, trenches or dips at the water's edge, which means you don't have to clamber out of the water looking like a bow-legged man walking on hot coals.

The sea here is perfect for wading and shallow and deep-water swimming, and only changes colour from blue to deep purple a quarter of a mile out when it reaches the Elson reef, which protects the in-shore waters.

I've visited a lot of beaches during my hard life as a travel writer, but have never found anything as close to perfection as the pink sand of this gifted location.

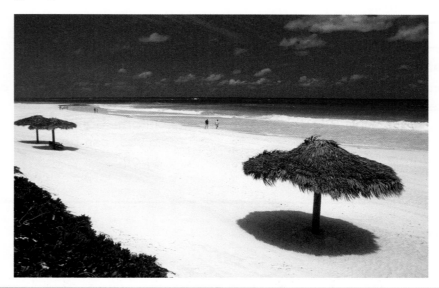

Putting it into practice

Look at the exam-style question below and read the two sample student answers.

Worked example

3 How does the writer use **language features** to **describe** the place and **persuade** people to go there?

Remember to:
- give some examples of language features to describe
- give some examples of language features to persuade.

(12 marks)

Writing about language

For a question like this you should:
- ☑ spend about 18 minutes
- ☑ read the source carefully and note effective use of language
- ☑ support all your points with evidence and a clear explanation focusing on **effect**.

Sample answer

The writer uses lots of language to inform. He tells the reader that the beach is in the Bahamas and that it is called North Beach.

He also tells you all the kinds of things you can do on the beach. He says it is perfection, which is persuasive.

✗ A vague point supported with reference to the text, but no explanation is given.

✗ Another vague point with no reference to the text or evidence.

This answer does not comment on language features. It simply notes them without explanation.

Improved sample answer

The writer begins with some informative facts about the beach. He tells the reader it is on 'Harbour Island's eastern shore' so that the reader knows where it is, making the article sound reliable and accurate. He goes on to say that it 'runs without interruption for three miles', which helps the reader imagine the beach. This fact is also persuasive because it makes the beach sound huge.

The writer uses a list of all the things that you will not find on the beach: 'cigarette butts, old beer bottles …', which makes the reader compare it with other beaches they might have been on, making this beach sound even more beautiful and unspoilt.

Note how this answer identifies the purpose of the text and the language features that support it.

✓ Effective comment on evidence.

✓ A perceptive comment on this fact, highlighting that it is both persuasive and informative.

✓ Another effective P-E-E paragraph commenting on effect.

Now try this

Complete the 'Improved sample answer', aiming to identify at least **two** more relevant points.

Remember to focus on specific language choices and comment closely on their effect.

Identifying presentational devices 1

Presentational devices affect how a text looks, either on screen or on paper. You will be asked about these in Section A, Question 4.

Colour

Colour is a significant presentational feature. It reflects mood and can even suggest your response. For example:

- black: evil, death, formality
- red: passion, fire, blood, danger
- orange: energy, warmth, happiness
- yellow: happiness, sunshine, cowardice

- green: nature, environment, jealousy
- blue: calm, cleanliness, sky, water
- purple: luxury, wealth, nobility
- white: purity, peace, winter

Headings attract the reader's attention.

Subheadings guide and direct the reader's understanding.

Images reflect meaning and influence the reader's response.

Plan ahead

Do
- Have your own revision timetable – start planning well before exams begin. Your teacher should be able to help.
- Make your books, notes and essays user-friendly. Use headings, highlighting and revision cards, and get tips on other revision techniques from teachers and friends with experience of exams. You could also consider buying revision guides.
- Take notes of the important points when revising. Try to answer the questions of past exam papers – explain answers to tricky questions to someone else.
- Everyone revises differently. Find out what routine suits you best - alone or with a friend or parent/carer; early morning or late at night; short, sharp bursts or longer sessions; with music or without noise.
- Ask for help from your teacher/learning mentor, parent/carer or a friend if there are things you don't understand.

Don't
- Don't leave revision to the last minute.
- Don't avoid revising subjects you don't like or find difficult.
- Don't forget that there is life beyond revision and exams.
- Don't cram ALL night before an exam.

Pamper yourself

Remember it's important to eat and sleep well.

Put yourself first – this is an important time for you. Try to talk to your family about how they can make studying a little easier for you – for example, by agreeing times when you can have your own space, when they will try to be a little quieter around the house and when you'd rather not be disturbed (except perhaps for the occasional treat, such as a drink or snack).

Don't revise all the time

Make sure you give yourself time each day to relax, taking breaks to do something you enjoy – watch TV, listen to music, read a book or go out for a walk.

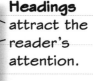

Font choice can help to emphasise certain points and can suggest a tone to the reader.

Remember:
- **font format** (using bold, italics or colour) can affect meaning and emphasise a point
- **images** can be drawings, photographs or other types of graphics
- **capital letters** make things stand out.

Now try this

Choose **three** presentational features of the leaflet extract above. Write **one** or **two** sentences about the effect of each one.

Identifying presentational devices 2

Structural devices are used to organise the text. You will be asked about these in Section A, Question 4.

Sections and boxes can be used to:
- highlight key information
- organise different sections of information.

Look out for information in bordered boxes or on blocks of coloured background.

Bullet points and numbering makes information quick and easy to understand. They can make a text look more interesting, and reduce the number of words.

Remember that numbered lists can also be used to sequence information or organise it in rank order, e.g. 'The Top Ten Reasons to …'.

Tables are used for large amounts of information, making it easier to read and understand.

Paragraphs break up blocks of text by organising them into sections.

Note that short paragraphs can make a text easier and quicker to read, and create a sense of pace.

Now try this

Choose a leaflet (one that has come through your letterbox, for example) or a webpage at random. Identify the presentational and structural features it uses to organise information and make it more accessible to the reader. Write **one** or **two** sentences about each one.

Using P-E-E to comment on presentational devices

In Section A, Question 4, you will explore the effect of presentational features in two texts. Point-Evidence-Explain will help you to organise your answers.

Answering questions

For Section A, Question 4, you will need to **explain** the effects of presentational features such as headlines, images, colour, etc. For example, you could explain the effect of the photograph in **Source 1**.

Headlines can grab attention.

Photographs can support both text and headlines.

Remember: when you are writing about how a text looks, your evidence might not be a quotation. It could be a description of presentation feature, e.g.

The text has a light grey background which suggests that

Source 1

A little competition

It's not a dangerous thing – school sports days can help nurture ambition in children

I am writing this having just returned from my daughter's sports day – at which, incidentally, she won the 100 metre sprint. You will have gathered from this that her school operates a pretty traditional kind of event.

You can use Point-Evidence-Explain to comment on presentational and structural devices.

A clear point about the headline.

Evidence and comment on its effect on the reader.

A second piece of evidence and a comment on its effect.

Worked example

4 Read **Source 1**. Explain how the text uses **presentational features** for effect. *(12 marks)*

The bold headline grabs the reader's attention. 'A little competition' does not give the reader much information so might make them want to read the article to find out more. It also uses a pun on the word 'little' as a school sports day is a competition for little people. The pun creates a humorous tone.

Now try this

Look again at **Source 1**. Write another Point-Evidence-Explain paragraph in which you explain how **either** the headline **or** the picture is effective.

Remember, in your exam you will need to compare the presentational features in two texts.

Commenting on headlines

Headlines and subheadings are important presentational features. When you write about them, you should focus closely on their specific effects.

Headlines are big and bold
They grab the reader's attention, making them want to read on ...
Howevever, these comments are rather obvious. There's a lot more you can say about headlines to write really good answers.

Does the **headline** intrigue the reader by not stating exactly what the story is about?

You should think about information it gives **and** the information it withholds.

Has the writer used alliteration or repetition to emphasise a key point or create impact?

Has a **subheading** been used to add more information?

You can develop your explanations by thinking more about a headline's language features.

Has the writer used a rhetorical question to make the reader curious and want to read on to discover the answer?

For example, a pun could create a humorous tone, or emotive language could add to the drama.

Has the writer used language that reflects the tone of the article?

Worked example

Read **Source 1**. What are the effects of the headline?

The headline clearly states what the article is about. It emphasises the key point that the jump was made 'without a parachute' to surprise and astonish the reader, adding the statistic that the jump was made from a height of '2,400 feet' to add to the effect.

Remember, you can:
- use more than one quotation to make your point
- point out more than one effect.

Source 1

Stuntman completes 2,400ft skydive without a parachute

A general point about the headline.

A short quotation.

A detailed comment focusing on effect.

Now try this

Look at **Source 2** opposite. Write a P-E-E paragraph about the headline and subheading, focusing on their effect.

Remember that P-E-E stands for Point-Evidence-Explain.

Source 2

Storm batters Birmingham
Seven families left homeless as torrential rain and 100mph winds strike city

Image and effect

Images do more than illustrate a text. They can influence your response to it, too. When you write about images, think carefully about the effect they have on the reader.

Image and impact

The **effect** of an image can sometimes be stronger than the text itself. The photograph on this website has been carefully chosen to **persuade** readers to give money to an animal charity.

This is what Benjie looked like when he was brought into our rescue centre. Your donations could save other dogs like Benjie. Please give generously.

Donate now

A # Teenage gangs run riot

B # Teens feel the pressure

Illustrating and influencing

Images can alter the way a reader responds to a text. For example, look at these three headlines and the images used to illustrate them.

Each one portrays teenagers in different ways.

Image A suggests that teenagers are intimidating and frightening.

Image B suggests that teenagers are hard-working and highly pressured by school work and exams.

Image C suggests that teenagers are generous and helpful, working hard to support their communities.

C # Saluting the army of teenage volunteers

Now try this

Write a description of the photo you would like to accompany an article you have written entitled:

The holiday of a lifetime!

Remember to include:
- what the photo will show
- whether it will have people in it (what they will be doing and how they look)
- what the weather will be like.

Comparing the presentation of two source texts

Section A, Question 4 asks you to compare the way that **two** source texts use presentational features for effect.

Comparing presentation

When you **compare** the presentation and its effects in two texts:

✓ **Do** make direct comparisons between the presentation features and their effect.

✗ **Don't** simply write about the presentation in one text and then the presentation in the other text.

✓ **Do** comment on the effect of language in a presentation feature such as a headline.

✗ **Don't** comment on the language of the source text generally. Focus on presentation.

You can **either** compare similar presentation features in the two texts and explore their effect …

For example, both texts feature the charities' logos.

Source 1

Source 2

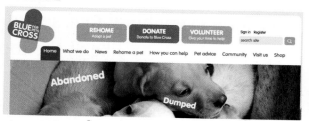

… **or** identify differences between the two texts and explore their different effects.

For example, both articles use images to persuade the reader to support their charity, but in different ways.

In **Source 1**, the image of a medal is used to emphasise that the soldiers the charity helps are heroes.

In **Source 2**, the logo is a blue cross reflecting the name of the charity.

In **Source 1**, the image shows a wounded soldier on a stretcher, emphasising the dangers which soldiers face.

In **Source 2**, the picture is of healthy animals that are very appealing. The words over the top of the image emphasise the neglect they can suffer.

Now try this

Use some of the ideas on this page, and some of your own.

1 Identify **one** further presentational feature used in each text.

2 Write **two** paragraphs comparing the use of presentational features in the two sources and its effects.

Putting it into practice

Read **Source** I then look at the question on the next page. (Note that in Section A, Question 4 of your exam, you will be asked to compare and comment on the effects of presentational features in **two texts**. Use this question to practise writing about presentation in just **one** text.)

Source 1

The secret footballer: undercover in the Premier League

Growing up on a council estate, all he wanted to do was play football. But a long career in the Premier League has made him question everything. Our secret footballer reveals what life is really like at the top of the game ...

A few years ago, I seriously considered giving up football. Sometimes, when the games are coming thick and fast, and you don't see your family, you aren't playing wonderfully well and the results are poor, it gets on top of you. I would later come to realise this was depression knocking at the door.

As a kid, I played football day and night – I used to take a ball to bed with me so that I could do keep-ups as soon as I woke up. Football held the possibility of glory and happiness, and an escape from the mundane life that came with growing up in a small town. I played for the best local teams, the county and district sides, and was known in our area as one of a crop of talented players who were emerging.

When I eventually signed with a team (for £500 a week, which was a fortune to me), I set about my newfound career with the overriding feeling that they'd

let someone in the door that perhaps they shouldn't have, an outsider into the inner sanctum. That feeling has never left me.

Putting it into practice

Look at the exam-style question below and read the extracts from two sample student answers.

Exploring presentational features

For a question like this you should:

- ☑ spend about 18 minutes
- ☑ look at the source carefully and note the presentational features
- ☑ support all your points with evidence and a clear explanation focusing on **effect**.

Worked example

4 Look at **Source 1**. Write about the way the text uses **presentational features** for effect.

Remember to:

- write about the way the source is **presented**
- explain the **effect** of the presentational features.
- compare the way they **look**.   *(12 marks)*

Sample answer

The headline is in a big, bold font which grabs the reader's attention. The image is quite interesting because you can't really see the person in it. It's mysterious so it grabs the reader's attention. The subheading gives more information than the heading so it makes you want to read on.

Make a note to avoid simple, obvious comments. The comments here could be about any headline.

✗ A vague comment needing much more detail about the effect of this image.

✗ Another very general comment that does not focus on any key words used in the headings or link back to the text in any way.

Improved sample answer

The headline grabs your attention because its in a large font and the words 'secret' and 'undercover' suggest to the reader that the article will give them some inside information about what it's really like to be a footballer in the Premier League. The subheading adds to this effect because it promises that the article will tell you what 'life is really like at the top of the game', which makes the reader feel that they will discover the truth.

✓ A clear point which makes a simple obvious comment but goes on to develop it.

✓ Picks out key words from the headline and comments on their effect.

✓ Clearly explains the headline's impact on the reader.

✓ Develops this idea further, using further evidence and explanation.

Now try this

Complete the 'Improved sample answer', focusing on the image.

Remember to:
- avoid simplistic comments (e.g. 'grabs the reader's attention' and 'makes the reader want to read on')
- comment on the use of language in the headline and subheading
- focus on the detail of the image and its effect.

45

Planning to compare presentation

Of all the questions in Section A, Question 4 is the most challenging. You will write a much better answer if you spend 4 or 5 minutes planning it.

Planning

One way to plan your answer is to look very carefully at both texts and note down similar presentation features. You can then identify some similarities and differences to explore.

Source 1

Guardian **Holiday Offers**

MURDER MYSTERY ON THE SEVERN VALLEY STEAM RAILWAY

A fun-filled short break to die for!
Picture the scene: The Severn Valley Railway's vintage steam train chugs its way through spectacular Worcestershire countryside. You're on board, enjoying a delicious three-course meal. But there's a twist to this tranquil tale – there's a murderer on the train, and it's up to you and your fellow guests to find out whodunnit!

- Bold headline: clearly tells reader what text is about.
- Image: shows what text is about to persuade reader.

Source 2

Auto Trader interview: James May

Captain Slow to some, a master of the motor to others, James May explains his passion for all things roadworthy, and some things that aren't …

What car do you currently drive?
I currently have a Bentley T2, a 1971 Rolls-Royce Corniche, a Jaguar XJS, a Porsche 911 and a Porsche Boxster S – the latter being the first car I ever purchased new.

You must have a few bikes too?
Yes, my garage is pretty full. I have a new Triumph Speed Triple, a Moto Guzzi V11Sport in lime green, a T3 California Guzzi,

- Bold headline: clearly tells reader what text is about.
- Image: reflects what text is about.
- Questions in bold to divide text up.

Now try this

Look at these sentence starters. Use each one to write a paragraph comparing the language techniques in the two sources and its effects.

1 The headlines for both texts …

2 Both texts use images to …

3 Unlike Source 1, Source 2 uses bold text to …

Don't try to write a little bit about every single presentation feature.

Do focus on two or three features and write about them in detail.

Answering a compare question

Writing about and comparing the presentation of two texts is difficult. You will fully demonstrate your understanding if you use an effective structure for your answer.

Structure

Aim to make direct comparisons.

You could **focus on one presentational feature** or its effect in the first text, then compare it to a similar feature or effect in the second text.

You could also **explore differences** – for example, writing about the different **images** in the two texts and how they affect your response.

Connectives

Use connectives to signpost the way through your answer.

For example, you could **signpost a similarity** using connectives like: 'Similarly …' or 'In the same way …'.

To **signpost a difference** you can use connectives like: 'However …' or 'Whereas …'.

Worked example

Write a brief introduction in one sentence summarising the two texts and their purposes.

Both texts are about … but **Source 1** aims to … while **Source 2** tries to …

Write about a presentational feature in **Source 1**, supported with evidence and an explanation of its effect on the reader.

Source 1 uses …

Similarly, **Source 2** uses …

Use a connective to link a point about a similar presentational feature in **Source 2**. Support this with evidence and explanation as well.

Both texts use images. For example, **Source 1** …

This makes the reader realise that …

On the other hand, **Source 2** uses its image to achieve a different effect …

EXAM SKILL

Remember that you can write about a difference in two texts – for example, different presentational features which have a similar effect.

Use this skill to help you improve the quality of your writing.

The writer has used a table in **Source 1**. He has done this to organise the information in the text to …

However, the writer of **Source 2** has organised the information in the text by …

Now try this

Look back at the two texts on page 46. Answer the exam question on the right, using the two texts.

Aim to use the ideas above to help you structure your answer.

4 Compare the way that both texts use **presentational features** for effect.
   • write about the way the sources are **presented**
   • explain the **effect** of the presentational features
   • compare the way they **look**.   *(12 marks)*

Putting it into practice

Look carefully at Source 1 and Source 2, then look at the question on the next page.

Source 1

CRACKING IDEAS COMPETITION

ENTER THIS YEAR'S COMPLETELY COSMIC CRACKING IDEAS SPACE COMPETITION!

ENTER THE COMPETITION

DOWNLOAD FORM

Whether you're into rocket launching science, lunar landscape art, deep space design or galactic gizmo technology this year's Cracking Ideas space competition is just for you. We need your super-sonic, space age Cracking Ideas rocketing their way to us. So ... go on ... go galactic ... get cracking!

HOW TO ENTER YOUR SPACE-AGE IDEAS

Create your cosmic entry:

You can enter this year's Cracking Ideas competition by simply downloading the Moon Bug pack. Or by requesting copies from Cracking Ideas, IPO, FREEPOST CF 4185, Newport, NP20 1ZZ or by emailing ideas@crackingideas.com. You'll be able to construct your special Moon Bug lunar contraption (complete with super-sonic pilots Wallace & Gromit) and then fill in your galactic winning ideas for patents, trade marks, design and copyright.

Alternatively you can use your own materials to make models, take photographs, draw plans or record your cosmic creation in just about any way you feel suits your innovative space-age Cracking Ideas.

All your space-age creations will star in the Cracking Ideas Gallery so keep checking back to see your cosmic entry feature.

UPLOAD YOUR IDEAS

Source 2

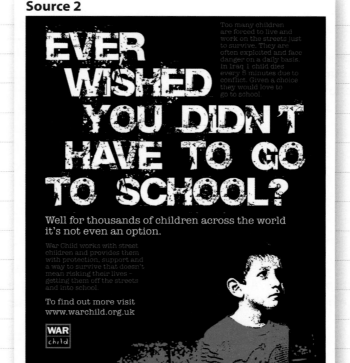

Putting it into practice

Look at the exam-style question below and read the extracts from two sample student answers.

Worked example

4   Look again at **Source 1** and **Source 2**. Compare the way that both texts use presentational features for effect.

Remember to:
- write about the way the sources are **presented**
- explain the **effect** of the presentational features
- compare the way they **look**.   *(12 marks)*

Exploring presentational features

For a question like this you should:
- ✓ spend about 18 minutes
- ✓ look at the sources carefully and note the presentational features
- ✓ support all your points with evidence and a clear explanation focusing on **effect**.

Sample answer

The image of Wallace and Gromit in Source 1 is funny and because it appeals to children would make them want to enter the competition.

The headings in Source 1 are in bold and <u>make you want to read on</u> and find out what the competition is about.

The background of the website is <u>light brown</u> but the poster in Source 2 <u>has a black background</u>.

> A reasonable point with limited comment on effect.

> ✗ A simple, obvious comment needing much more detail about the effect of this feature.

> ✗ Simply describes presentational features without comment so would achieve no marks.

> There is only one reference to Source 2 and no detailed comparison of the two texts.

Improved sample answer

> A clear, simple point that is developed in the explanation, focusing on effect.

The image in Source 1 shows Wallace and Gromit who are known as great inventors. This might inspire children to think of their own inventions and enter the competition. <u>However,</u> the image in Source 2 is much more disturbing. It shows a perfectly normal child but, on this poster with its text about children dying, <u>makes the reader feel worried</u> for him and all the other children in danger.

The website uses brown and purple as its main colours which are warm and comfortable colours. The poster however is mainly black and red which suggest danger, blood and death. This makes the website inviting and the poster quite alarming.

> ✓ A connective signals a comparison.
> ✓ Clearly explains the feature's impact on the reader.

> Another clear point, focusing on a comparison of the two texts' presentation and its effect.

Now try this

Complete the 'Improved sample answer', commenting on more presentational features.

Remember to:
- avoid simplistic comments (e.g. 'grabs the reader's attention' and 'makes it stand out')
- comment on the use of presentation, not language
- check you have commented on the effect of each feature you write about.

Reading the questions

Before you get stuck into your revision for Section B: Writing, you need to know:

☑ **how to pick out the key information in the questions**

☑ how long you have to spend on each answer.

You need to read each question in the exam very carefully to make sure you know exactly what the question is asking you to do. This page will help you practice this.

What the questions tell you

The questions in **Section B: Writing** tell you what you need to know in order to write an effective answer. Look at this example. Don't try to answer the question – just get used to the style.

This tells you your **audience** – who you are writing for. It suggests you are writing for students / parents / teachers.

> **6** Your school or college magazine is inviting students to write an article with the title 'Money isn't everything', Write an article **arguing** for or against this point of view.
>
> Remember to:
> • write an **article**
> • use language to **argue**.   *(24 marks)*

This tells you your **form** – what kind of text you are writing. Here, it is a magazine article.

This tells you the **topic** – what you are writing about. Here, it is the importance of money compared to other things.

This tells you your **purpose** – what your text must achieve. Here, you need to argue your point of view.

What the questions don't tell you

The exam questions will **not** remind you about the assessment objectives being used to assess your writing, so you need to remember what they are.

Communicate clearly, effectively and imaginatively, using and adapting forms and selecting vocabulary appropriate to task and purpose in ways that engage the reader.

For this assessment objective you should:
• express your ideas clearly
• use the right form (letter, newspaper article, etc.)
• choose effective and appropriate vocabulary to keep the reader interested.

Organise information and ideas into structured and sequenced sentences, paragraphs and whole texts, using a variety of linguistic and structural features to support cohesion and overall coherence.

For this assessment objective you should:
• plan and structure your work in sentences and paragraphs
• use connectives and other devices to link your ideas and make them easy to follow.

Use a range of sentence structures for clarity, purpose and effect, with accurate punctuation and spelling.

For this assessment objective you should:
• vary the length and types of sentences you use
• spell and punctuate accurately.

Now try this

Look at this exam-style question:

> **5** A national newspaper is inviting students to write an **article** called 'Dream School'. Write your article, **describing** the perfect school.   *(16 marks)*

Don't try to answer this question. Instead, note down:
• the audience it is asking you to write for
• the purpose your text should achieve
• the form it is asking you to use
• the topic it is asking you to write about.

The questions and planning your exam time

In Section B, you will be given **two** writing tasks. You must complete **both of them**.

- **Question 5** asks you to complete a piece of writing to **inform, explain or describe**. For example:

- **Question 6** asks you to complete a piece of writing to **persuade** or **argue** a point of view. For example:

> 5　A national newspaper is inviting students to write an **article** called 'Dream School'. Write your article, **describing** the perfect school.
>
> Remember to:
> - write an **article**
> - use language to **describe**.　　(16 marks)

> 6　'Watching television is a waste of everybody's time.' Write an **article** for a magazine of your choice **arguing** for or against this view.
>
> Remember to:
> - write an **article**
> - argue your **point of view.**　　(24 marks)

> 5　Write a **leaflet** aimed at teenagers **explaining** why GCSEs are important.
>
> Remember to:
> - write a **leaflet**
> - use language to **explain**.　　(16 marks)

> 6　Write a **blog** for a travel website, **persuading** visitors to come and spend some time exploring your local area.
>
> Remember to:
> - write a **blog**
> - use language to **persuade**.　　(24 marks)

How much time to spend on each question?

You have **one hour** to complete both writing tasks. The instructions on the exam paper advise you to:

- spend 25 minutes on **Question 5**, which is worth 16 marks
- spend 35 minutes on **Question 6**, which is worth 24 marks.

So you could organise your time like this:

Question 5: 25 mins		Question 6: 35 mins	
Plan the answer:	5 mins	Plan the answer:	5 mins
Write the answer:	17 mins	Write the answer:	27 mins
Check the answer:	3 mins	Check the answer:	3 mins
	25 mins		35 mins

Now try this

Look at one of the Question 6 exam-style questions above. Don't try to answer it. Instead note down:
- the audience it is asking you to write for
- the purpose your text should achieve
- the form it is asking you to use
- the topic it is asking you to write about.

Writing for an audience

The writing tasks will often tell you the audience you are writing for. You need to make your writing appealing, appropriate and accessible **to that audience**.

Audience

The audience you are writing for may be clearly **stated** in the task:

> Write a **guide** for Year 7 students **informing** them about …

In this example, you need to write for an audience of 11–12 year-old school students.

Or the audience may be **implied** in the task:

> Write an **article** for your school or college magazine in which you …

In this example, you would need to write for people who will see a school magazine (i.e. an audience of students, teachers and parents).

Formality and standard English

You will need to use formal language and standard English for most of the writing tasks and audiences you will be given in the exam. (Only use informal language where it is appropriate for the purpose and audience of your writing.) So you should avoid:

- slang (e.g. I was gutted)
- non-standard English (e.g. I haven't never done that)
- abbreviations (e.g. You shouldn't)
- text language (e.g. Ha ha LOL).

Language and audience

You may be asked to write for a teenage audience or for younger children.

> Write a **guide** for teenagers, **explaining** how …

If you are asked to write a text for teenagers you may want to include some slang.

> If I use some slang, I may make a younger audience feel like I am talking to them in their own language.

> If I use too much slang and other informal language, I may make my writing seem careless and unreliable.

Think about your audience's age, and the language they would use and understand.

If you are writing for an audience of Year 7 students, you should choose appropriate, accessible language like:

> Don't leave homework until the night before it's due in!

rather than:

> It is highly inadvisable to delay the completion of independent study tasks until shortly before the deadline for submission.

Worked example

5 Write an **article** for your school or college website, **informing** readers about GCSEs and explaining why they are important.
(16 marks)

You reckon you've got ages until your GCSEs. You reckon, so what? But I'm telling you, you're gonna be doing GCSEs before you know it.

You need to start working on them right now!

This answer is far too informal. The text should be appropriate for students and parents – and formal enough to suggest the information is reliable.

Now try this

Rewrite the opening paragraph of the student answer opposite, using formal standard English appropriate to the audience suggested in the task.

Writing for a purpose: inform and explain

When you write with the purpose of informing and explaining, there are a number of techniques you can use. These will help you organise your writing, engage your audience and achieve your purpose.

Headings and subheadings

- Use headings to organise texts to help find information.
- Use subheadings to help pick out key areas to include when planning writing.

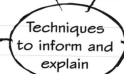

Techniques to inform and explain

Facts and statistics

These suggest that the information in a text can be trusted. Use facts and statistics:

- from the source texts in Section A: Reading
- you already know that are relevant to the writing task.

Facts and statistics are supposed to be believable, for instance, this seems believable: 'Our school recycles nearly 70% of its waste paper' and this less believable 'Our school recently completed a sponsored walk which raised over £1 million for charity.'

Language

Because information texts are factual and formal avoid using in your writing:

- figurative language
- rhetorical devices.

Structure

Information and explanation texts are usually organised chronologically. To signpost this to the reader use connectives:

- First ...
- Next ...
- Then ...
- Finally ...

Tone

Aim for a formal tone to suggest to the reader that the information is unbiased and reliable. Use:

- formal language
- Standard English
- third person (he, she, they).

EXAM SKILL

You can still use a simile, some alliteration or other language devices – but always stick to the purpose of the text. Don't lose focus and start to persuade or argue when you are supposed to be informing or explaining.

Use this skill to help you improve the quality of your writing.

Now try this

Look at this exam-style question and then complete tasks 1 to 4 opposite:

5 Write a **guide** to appear in a magazine for parents informing them about the difficulties of being a teenager today and **explaining** how parents can help them.
(16 marks)

1 Write down **three** subheadings you could use to organise your writing.

2 Write a sentence describing the tone you would use in this task, and how you would achieve it.

3 Write down any facts or statistics you could include in your writing.

4 Write the **first two** sentences of your answer.

Writing for a purpose: describe

When you write with the purpose of describing something, there are a number of techniques you can use. These will help you engage your reader and achieve your purpose.

The five senses

When you write to describe a place or an experience, you want the reader to experience what it was like to *be* there.

The only way we can experience anything is through our senses:

sight · sound · Five senses · smell · touch · taste

Often writers focus on the sense of sight. By using the other four senses as well, you can create **much** more vivid descriptions.

Figurative language

Figurative language, or **imagery**, can create an image in the reader's mind. It includes language devices such as:

* similies
* metaphors
* personification.

Used sparingly and imaginatively, figurative language can help to create rich and powerful descriptions.

See page 27

for more on figurative language

Remember to avoid clichés (well-known, overused figurative language). Describing someone as 'cool as a cucumber' or a landscape as 'flat as a pancake' does **not** demonstrate imagination and originality.

Feelings

Describing the narrator's feelings can bring descriptive writing to life. It helps the reader understand and share those feelings. Remember to **show** the reader how the narrator feels, rather than **tell** them. For example, it is much more effective to write:

✓ A smile spread across my face and warm satisfaction rose from my stomach to the tips of my ears.

than:

✗ I felt really, really happy.

Language choice

In descriptive writing, it can be tempting to use as much descriptive language as possible. It's much more effective to use fewer words which you have chosen really carefully. Try to use one precise descriptive word, rather than three vague words. For example:

✓ I danced across the road

creates a much more immediate and powerful picture than:

✗ I walked cheerfully with a spring in my step across the road as though I were dancing.

Think about the **quality** of your descriptive language, not the **quantity**.

Now try this

Write the **first** paragraph of your response to this question.

Describe a time when you were frightened.

You should choose your language for quality, not quantity. In your writing, try to use:
* at least two different senses
* a description of your feelings
* at least one example of figurative language.

Writing for a purpose: argue and persuade

When you write with the purpose of arguing and persuading, there are a number of techniques you can use to help you engage your reader and achieve your purpose.

Key points

The power of your persuasion relies on the strength of your key points. To argue your opinion, choose key points which highlight:
- why you are right
- why those who disagree are wrong.

To persuade your reader, choose key points which highlight:
- what is **wrong** with the way things are
- how your ideas will make things **better**.

Evidence

Always support **each** of your key points with convincing evidence. This could be:
- a fact or statistic
- an expert opinion
- an example from your own experience.

Connectives

Use connectives to signpost the path your argument is going to follow.

See page 68 for more on connectives

To build your argument, you could use:
- furthermore ...
- moreover ...
- additionally ...

To introduce counter-arguments, you can use:
- however ...
- on the other hand ...

To explain your argument, you could use:
- consequently ...
- therefore ...

Counter-arguments

Think about the ways in which your reader might disagree with you – and then point out why they are wrong. This is an effective way of discussing opposing ideas. For example:

Your reader may have different ideas about the way things are or the way to make things better. You can dismiss these ideas using a counter-argument.

Some people think that teenagers are lazy and uncaring. But it is the media who give us these negative images, and ignore all those teenagers who work hard, behave responsibly and even raise money for good causes.

Rhetorical devices

These can add great power to your argument.

To engage and influence your reader, you can use:
- rhetorical questions
- direct address.

To add power to your argument, use:
- repetition
- lists
- alliteration
- contrast
- patterns of three
- emotive language
- hyperbole.

See pages 25 and 26 for more on rhetorical devices

Now try this

Note down some ideas which you could use in your response to the exam-style question below:

Aim to:
- note down three key points, supported with evidence
- identify and dismiss a counter-argument
- write three sentences using three different rhetorical devices.

6 Write an **article** for your school magazine **persuading** students to enter a talent show you are organising.   *(24 marks)*

Putting it into practice

Before you start thinking about the writing tasks and how to complete them, work out how long you should spend on each question.

Here is one student's exam plan for Section B: Writing. Now write their planning and checking time as well.

Timing

Q5: 25 mins   (10.00–10.25am)

Q6: 35 mins   (10.25–11.00am)

Reading the questions

When you first look at **Section B: Writing** you should:

- ☑ plan your time – you have one hour
- ☑ read each question carefully
- ☑ note the task's purpose, audience and form
- ☑ note the key features you need to remember for the text you are going to write.

Look carefully at each question and make sure you identify exactly what the question is asking you to do. Look at how this student has highlighted the key features of this question:

Implies audience

Purpose 1 + topic

5   A local newspaper is inviting entries for a writing competition, asking writers to write an article describing the most important day of their life so far. Write your entry.
Remember to:
- write an **article**
- use language to **describe**. *(16 marks)*

Form: article

Now try this

6   The head of your school or college has written a letter to staff, students and parents announcing that the school playing fields are to be sold and the money used to build a new science block and school library. Write a **letter** to the head, **arguing** for or against this idea.
Remember to:
- write a **letter**
- use language to **argue**.
(24 marks)

Look closely at the exam-style question above. Pick out the key information about:
- which audience to write for
- the form in which you should write
- the purpose your writing should achieve
- the topic of your writing.

Form: letters and emails

You may be asked to write a letter or an email for either of the writing tasks in your exam. Show that you know what you are doing by using the key features of the form in which you have been asked to write – and by setting them out correctly.

In **formal letters**:

- Your address goes in the top right-hand corner.
- Put the date underneath your address.
- The person you are writing to and their address goes on the left, lower down.
- **Yours** has a capital letter – but **sincerely** and **faithfully** do not.
- Print your name beneath your signature.

If you use the name of the person you are writing to here, then end with **Yours sincerely**. If you use 'Dear Sir/Madam', then end with **Yours faithfully**. A letter to a friend or relative might end less formally with **Lots of love** or **Cheers**.

17 Jordan Avenue
Brimworth
Brimshire BX17 M3U

17 February 2013

The Editor
Brimshire Gazette
17 High Street
Brimworth
Brimshire
BX1 8TT

Dear Sir/Madam

I am writing to express my concerns at the

and hope that it never happens again.

Yours faithfully

Andrew Aidan

Formal emails use some of the same features as formal letters.

- Note that postal addresses and the date are not included in emails.
- Like a formal letter, you begin **Dear ...**
- You can end with **Yours sincerely** or with something a little less formal.

Dear Mr Patel
I am writing to apply for the position advertised in the Brimshire Gazette.

I look forward to hearing from you.

Best wishes
Andrew Aidan.

In **informal emails**:

- Postal addresses and the date are not included.
- You can begin Hi or Hello ...
- You can end with something much less formal.

Hi Annie
Mum told me that you were thinking of doing some volunteer work so I thought I'd write and

Lots of love
Andy

Now try this

Look back at the letters and emails on this page. Make a list of the key features of each of these forms.

Form: articles

You may be asked to write a newspaper, magazine or web article for either of the writing tasks in your exam.

The headline gives enough information to intrigue the reader – and may use a pun, alliteration, repetition, rhetorical question, etc.

The subheading gives more information, drawing the reader in.

The truth about lying: it's the hands that betray you, not the eyes

By analysing videos of liars, the team found there was no link to their eye movements

ADAM SHERWIN

The eyes don't lie.

It is often claimed that even the most stone-faced liar will be betrayed by an unwitting eye movement.

But new research suggests that "lying eyes", which no fibber can avoid revealing, are actually a myth.

Verbal hesitations and excessive hand gestures may prove a better guide to whether a person is telling untruths, according to research conducted by Professor Richard Wiseman.

Many psychologists believe that when a person looks up to their right they are likely to be telling a lie. Glancing up to the left, on the other hand, is said to indicate honesty.

But the experts are wrong, according to Prof Wiseman, a psychologist from the University of Hertfordshire: 'The results of the first study revealed no relationship between lying and eye movements, and the

In the exam, you don't have to write your headline in bold block writing. Your normal handwriting will do.

The writer's name, or byline.

Opening paragraphs summarise the key points to engage the reader.

Later paragraphs add more detail.

Quotations from experts or people involved in the story add interest and authenticity.

Now try this

Look at this exam-style question.

6 Write an **article** for your school or college magazine **persuading** students to enter a talent show you are organising.
Remember to:
- write an **article**
- use language to **persuade**. *(24 marks)*

Write the first **three** paragraphs of your article. Try to:
- sum up your key ideas in paragraph 1
- add more detail in paragraph 2
- use a quotation in paragraph 3.

Form: information sheets

You may be asked to write an information sheet for either of the writing tasks in your exam.

Headings and subheadings

Headings and subheadings can engage the reader's attention. They can also guide the reader through the information available.

Bullet points and numbered lists

Lists can provide a lot of information in a short space. Numbered lists can be used to show ranking, or a chronological sequence of events.

Worked example

5 Produce a **leaflet**, **informing** other students about a sport or activity which your school or college offers.
Remember to:
- write an **article**
- use language to **inform**.

(16 marks)

Learning the drums

Five great reasons to learn the drums

1
2
3
4
5

Buying a drum kit

You don't need to spend a fortune to learn the drums. Just buy a pair of sticks and a practice pad!

Text boxes can be used to highlight key information. Remember, you can use boxes, tables and charts to present large amounts of information quickly and clearly.

Getting started
The first things you will learn are:
-
-
-

Playing in a band

Now try this

Plan your own response to the exam-style question above. Note down:
- a heading
- **four** or **five** key subheadings
- any text boxes, tables, charts or lists you would include.

Remember that:
- information sheets often use subheadings to organise the text and guide the reader
- letters or articles written to inform the reader usually do not.

Putting it into practice

Look at the exam-style question below and read the two sample student answers.

Worked example

6 Your local council is asking all young people in the area to give up two or three hours a month to do some voluntary work. Young people will have the choice of helping at a care home for the elderly, litter picking, or clearing a local woodland to encourage wildlife.

Write a **letter** to your local council **arguing** for or against this idea.

Remember to:
- write a **letter**   • use language to **argue**.   *(24 marks)*

For each writing question you should:

☑ spend a minute or two reading the question carefully

☑ note the form, purpose, audience and topic for the task

☑ check you have included all the key features of the form.

Sample answer

10 High Street
Townville
TO13 2UX

Dear Council
I am writing to tell you that I think it's a really bad idea to ask young people to help out at

So I hope you will bear this in mind.
Yours
Bill Bradshaw

✓ Includes own address, correctly positioned.

✗ Does not include date, or address of the person he is writing to.

✓ Appropriately formal

✗ Inappropriately informal

Improved sample answer

27 Elm Avenue
Bradcaster
Brimshire
BX14 7PI
28 March 2013

Ms P Grimley
Brimshire County Council
PO Box 17
Brimforth
Brimshire BX1 1AA

Dear Ms Grimley
I am writing regarding the council's recent decision to

Yours sincerely
Alice Trimm

EXAM SKILL

Using the key features of a form will not improve your answer as much as focusing on purpose, audience, language, etc., but it will help.

Use this skill to help you improve the quality of your writing.

All the key features of this letter have been included.

✓ Own address

✓ Date written

✓ Address written to

✓ Appropriate formal salutation

✓ Correct, formal sign-off

Now try this

Write the first and last paragraphs to the exam-style question above.

Remember to include all the key features of a formal letter.

Planning an answer: describe

Planning is the only way to produce a well-structured piece of writing, full of relevant, imaginative ideas and carefully crafted language.

Describing a scene

Describe a primary school at the start of a day.

For a question like this, picture the scene in your mind. Divide the scene into sections, then ask yourself:

- What is nearest to you?
- What is beyond that?
- What's in the distance?
- What's furthest from you?

Use the answers to these questions to structure three or four paragraphs:

Plan
1 Parents waving, driving away.
2 Iron gates, playground, hopscotch.
3 School buildings, teacher at window.
4 Clouds gathering, rain coming.

Describing an event

Describe a time when you changed your plans.

You can describe this event in chronological order:

Plan
1 Woke up – excited – day out with Ryan.
2 Ryan rings – dumped me.
3 Sulking. Phone rings. Best friend wants me to go on holiday with her.

or you can start with a dramatic moment and fill in the gaps later:

Plan
1 Ryan rings – dumped me.
2 Flashback – woke up excited – day out with Ryan.
3 Sulking. Phone rings. Best friend wants me to go on holiday with her.

Don't worry if you can't remember a suitable event in your life. Make it up!

Gathering ideas

When you've got the basic structure of your piece organised, think about how you can add to your plan using:

- the five senses
- your feelings
- details to create mood or atmosphere
- language for effect.

1 Parents waving / driving away sound of chatter, engines, smell of exhaust

2 Iron gates cold grey, playground, hopscotch – screams / laughter of kids, one crying

3 School buildings, teacher at window building has blank windows like dead eyes; teacher has angry, narrow eyes, menacing

Plan

4 Clouds gathering, rain coming thunder rumbles, kids scatter like litter on the wind, playground empty, bell rings

Now try this

Choose one of the writing tasks at the top of this page. Plan **four** or **five** paragraphs using your own ideas. Create a mind map or spidergram to bring all your ideas together.

Remember:
- you only have **25 minutes** to plan, write and check this task – so aim for **three** or **four** paragraphs of well-crafted writing
- quality is rewarded – quantity is not
- descriptions needn't be action-packed.

61

Planning an answer: inform or explain

Familiarise yourself with how to compile a plan so that you will not find it a problem in the exam.

Informing or explaining, or both

Worked example

5 Write a **letter** to your local council **informing** them about the facilities for teenagers in your local area and explaining how they could be improved.
Remember to:
• write a **letter**
• use language to **explain**. *(16 marks)*

Plan an introduction that tells your reader what are you writing and why they should read it.

Gather key points to help you organise your ideas. Number your subheadings or key points, putting them in a logical order.

> You might want to change your order once you have written your plan.

Add ideas to develop your subheadings or key points. You may decide to combine two key points in one paragraph or divide one key point into two paragraphs.

Sample answer

<u>Plan</u>
• Intro
  • Not enough facilities.
  • Need to improve them.
  • Stop teenagers causing problems in town.

2 What do teenagers do?
  • Hang around town.
  • A few cause trouble.
  • Crowds of teens can be intimidating.

1 What is there to do?
  • Youth club once a week.
  • Cinema / bowling alley but both expensive and both 5 miles away.

3 What can be done?
  • Youth club open two or three nights a week.
  • Volunteers to do it up.
  • Develop waste ground next to station – skate park.
  • Teen council to get ideas / suggestions.

Now try this

Look at this exam-style question:

5 What is the one thing which would make the biggest difference to teenagers' lives?
Write an **article** for a magazine of your choice **explaining** what the 'one thing' is and why it would make such a difference.
Remember to:
• write an **article**
• use language to **explain**. *(16 marks)*

Plan your answer, creating a list, mind map or spidergram to bring all your ideas together.
Aim to plan **three** or **four** paragraphs.

EXAM SKILL

Remember, even though you will not always include subheadings when you write an information or explanation text, you can still use them to help you plan your writing.

> Use this skill to help you improve the quality of your writing.

Planning an answer: argue or persuade

Planning an answer is the only way to produce a well-structured piece of writing, full of relevant, imaginative ideas and carefully crafted language. It is particularly important when writing to plan your argument so it is logically constructed.

Worked example

6 'Watching television is a waste of everybody's time.' Write an **article** for a magazine of your choice which **persuades** your readers that this statement is right or wrong.

Remember to:
- write an **article**
- use language to **persuade**.   (24 marks)

If the question gives you a choice, decide whether you are **for** or **against**. Remember to give your writing a title that reflects your point of view.

Write your introduction, telling the reader what the situation is at the moment, and why that is a problem they need to think about.

Add some evidence to support each key point you make. **Plan key points** by gathering together all the different ideas you can think of that support your viewpoint.

Choose and sequence the most persuasive points. You will probably only need two or three key points.

Don't stop when you've thought of three ideas. Think of more, reject weaker ideas, then put the strong ideas in a logical order.

Add a counter-argument that gives an opposing viewpoint. Then say why you disagree.

Plan a conclusion – your final point to hammer home your argument.

Sample answer

Plan: TV is stealing your life
Intro
100s of channels run all day and all night
Average person watches 4 hours a day –
a quarter of their waking life!

2 TV is passive not active
Evidence: my sister – hours spent staring, doing nothing. Overweight and silent, TV is killing her brain and body.

3 TV is addictive
Once you start, it's difficult to turn off
Evidence: watch least worst programme, not choosing what to watch

Don't be afraid to cross out some of your ideas.

~~Advertising is annoying~~
~~10/15 mins of it every hour — they want my~~
~~money!~~

1 Families don't talk anymore
Evidence: Mine eats dinner in silence in front of the telly.

4 Some say it's educational and entertaining
It can be both – but how often? More often it's neither – e.g. Big Brother.

Conclusion
Most telly is a waste of time for everyone. Choose what you want to watch – then turn it off.

Now try this

Write a plan for the **other** side of the argument in the exam-style question above, arguing that television is not a waste of time.

63

Beginnings

Starting a piece of writing can be difficult. Know what you want to write, or you will be in danger of writing one or two boring paragraphs before you really get going.

An effective opening

Your first paragraph of any writing task – and your first sentence in particular – needs to grab the reader's interest and attention. You could use one or more of these five ideas.

- A bold and / or controversial statement:

> Experimenting on animals is a cruel necessity.

- A relevant quotation:

> 'One small step for a man, one giant leap for mankind.'
>
>   (Neil Armstrong, first man on the moon)

- A shocking or surprising fact or statistic:

> 99 per cent of the species that have ever lived on Planet Earth are now extinct.

- A rhetorical question:

> Why do adults think they are always right?

- A short, relevant, **interesting** anecdote:

> When I was seven, my parents bought me a dog. This was when I first realised that ...

EXAM SKILL

Avoid telling the reader what you are going to write about:
In this essay I am going to argue that television is not a waste of time.
Just write it:
Television is informative, educational and interesting.

Use this skill to help you improve the quality of your writing.

Introducing your topic

After your opening sentence, go on to introduce what you are writing about.

Sample answer

> ... The average person spends <u>a quarter of their waking life watching television</u>. Are they making good use of their time? Or is television sucking the life out of them, killing them slowly with its mind-numbing mediocrity?

A surprising statistic shocks the reader and grabs their attention. Here, it invites the reader to compare how long they spend watching TV.

Two questions engage the reader, and present the two sides of the argument. The second question makes it clear which side the writer is on.

Now try this

Look at this exam-style question:

> 6 'There is more to school than passing exams.' Write an **article** for a magazine of your choice which **persuades** your readers that this statement is right or wrong.   *(24 marks)*

1 Write **three** possible opening sentences that would grab the reader's attention from the start.

2 Choose the best one then complete your introduction, explaining what you are writing about.

Endings

Plan your conclusion before you start writing. The final paragraph of your writing should leave your reader with a lasting impression.

Summing up

The final paragraph or conclusion to a text can be used to sum up your ideas – but avoid repeating them. Instead, aim to sum up and emphasise your central idea. You could use one or more of these things.

> Avoid introducing your conclusion with phrases like:
> - In conclusion …
> - To summarise …

End on a vivid image: a picture that lingers in the reader's mind.

> A homeless person sits cold and alone in a shop doorway. As you pass by, you look into her eyes. She can't be older than 15.

End on a warning: what will happen if your ideas are not acted on?

> Within 50 years, the world will have changed beyond all recognition – and our children will blame us for what has happened.

End on a happy note: emphasise how great things will be if your ideas are acted on.

> Ours could be the generation that made the difference.

End on a thought-provoking question: leave the reader thinking.

> For how long can we ignore what is staring us in the face?

Refer back to your introduction, but don't repeat it.

> I still have that dog – and he's still incredibly badly behaved. But if I hadn't …

End on a call to action: make it clear what you want the reader to do.

> Don't just sit there. Get up, get out and make it happen.

Worked example

6 'Watching television is a waste of everybody's time.' Write an article for a magazine of your choice which persuades your readers that this statement is right or wrong.

Remember to:
- write an **article**
- use language to **persuade**.   (24 marks)

> Remember that questions engage the reader with the issue – how does it relate to their own life?

How many hours of television have you watched this week? What else could you have done with those hours? Television has turned us all into spectators - and while we're glued to the box, our lives are ticking away, wasted and unused. It's time to stop watching. It's time to start taking part.

A warning.

A final, powerful call to action.

Now try this

Look at the exam-style question opposite. Choose **one or more** of the above techniques to write a powerful conclusion.

6 'There is more to school than passing exams.' Write an **article** for a magazine of your choice which **persuades** your readers that this statement is right or wrong.

Remember to:
- write an **article**
- use language to **persuade**.   (24 marks)

Putting it into practice

Look at the exam-style question below and read the two sample student plans.

Worked example

5   Write an **article** for a travel website, **describing** a place of interest in your area.
Remember to:
- write an **article**
- use language to **describe**.   (16 marks)

Planning

For each writing question you should:
- ☑ spend 3–5 minutes gathering ideas
- ☑ organise and sequence your ideas
- ☑ think about how you will introduce and conclude your writing.

Sample answer

Bradcaster Park
- Good, fun, interesting.
- Playground for kids.
- Lake
-

✗ Some language ideas but undeveloped / unambitious.

✗ Some ideas gathered, but more needed.

Make sure you provide a range of details for questions like this. In this plan there is no detail added about the lake, the information about the park is not sequenced, and there is no introduction or conclusion.

Sample answer

- Industrial revolution exhibits. ③

- Roman coins found – story of man and metal detector. ①

Some fossils

Brimshire County Museum

- Medieval village reconstruction – get involved in old crafts, etc. ②

Note that the answer is logically sequenced in historical order. Remember that effectively sequencing your ideas will improve your writing.

✓ Ideas gathered.

✓ Detail added.

✓ Less detailed idea discarded.

Intro: tells you all about the area and its history in last 2,000 years.

Conclusion: what life was really like here over the centuries.

Now try this

Plan your answer to the exam-style question above and write an opening paragraph.

Remember to:
- gather, organise and sequence your ideas
- plan your introduction and conclusion.

Paragraphing

The best answers are organised into paragraphs. They help structure your writing, making it easier for the reader to follow your thinking and absorb your ideas.

Paragraphs

Use paragraphs to divide your writing into clear points. Paragraphs help the reader follow your ideas and make the whole text more accessible.

Planning can help you paragraph your writing. Make a clear plan, setting out all the points you want to make. Each time you start a new point, start a new paragraph.

one paragraph = one point

Paragraphing for effect

In most cases you should start a new paragraph each time you start a new point. However, you can use shorter paragraphs for effect: to emphasise a point or create a dramatic pause.

> News articles often use short paragraphs of just one or two sentences. This creates a sense of pace and keeps the reader 'moving' through the text.

> Some people argue there is no proof that global warming is caused by human activity. They argue that global warming would be happening anyway and there is nothing we can do about it.
>
> This attitude will end in disaster.
>
> Doing nothing is precisely what created the problem in the first place. While we sit and wait and see what happens, time is running out.

Structuring paragraphs: argue and persuade

Use Point-Evidence-Explain to structure paragraphs in a piece of writing to argue or persuade.

- A short, clear **point**.
- **Evidence** to support the point.
- **Explains** how the point and evidence are relevant to the main idea.

> Britain's weather is changing. Barely a month goes by without it being declared the wettest, the driest, the hottest, the coldest, or the windiest month on record. Our weather is clearly becoming more extreme, and is likely to become even more so. How long can we ignore this before we act?

Structuring paragraphs: inform, explain, describe

Start each paragraph with a **topic sentence** – a sentence that clearly introduces the reader to the content of this paragraph. Use the remainder of the paragraph to develop and add detail to the topic sentence.

- Topic sentence
- Detail / development

> Our school has made a huge effort to recycle its waste. Every classroom has a bin just for waste paper which is collected each week by student volunteers. In the canteen, we sort our rubbish into plastics, tin cans, and food waste. Even the staff room has three different bins so teachers can recycle!

Now try this

Write the next paragraph to either of the student answers above.

Using connectives

Connectives help to guide the reader through your ideas. They work like signposts, showing the reader the direction your ideas are taking. They can be used in a variety of ways to improve your writing.

Adding an idea

• Moreover ...
• Furthermore ...
• In addition ...
• Not only ... but also

This will not solve the situation. **Moreover**, it could make it worse.

Not only is this likely to interrupt students' learning, **but also** adds to their stress levels.

Explaining

• Because
• Therefore
• Consequently

Science suggests that the teenage brain needs more sleep to help it grow and develop. **Consequently**, we spend longer in bed.

Teenagers' attitudes and actions are constantly challenged. It is **therefore** unsurprising that they sometimes challenge those who challenge them.

Illustrating

• For example
• For instance
• Such as

Problems, **such as** vandalism and graffiti and, continue to grow.

Emphasising

• In particular
• Especially
• Significantly

Significantly, these problems increased when the youth club was shut down.

Comparing

• Similarly
• In the same way

It has been argued that an animal's life is not as important as that of a human being. **Similarly**, it has been argued that animals should be exploited for our food, health and wealth.

Contrasting

• However
• On the other hand
• ... whereas ...

When using a contrasting connective, it's often a good idea to start a new paragraph.

Some young people are strongly and unthinkingly influenced by the role models which the media provides. **However**, many are not.

Now try this

Look at the exam-style question opposite. Write as many sentences as you can on this topic, using a different connective in each one.

5 Choose a topic you know a lot about – for example, a hobby, a sport, a person, etc. Write a **guide informing** the reader about your topic.
Remember to:
• write a **guide**
• use language to **inform**.   *(16 marks)*

Putting it into practice

Look at the exam-style question below and read the two sample student answers.

Worked example

6 Your local newspaper is running a campaign to encourage older people to learn about and use computers. Write an **article** for the newspaper **persuading** the elderly to find out more about computers.

Remember to:
  • write an **article**
  • use language to **persuade**.   *(24 marks)*

Paragraphing and connectives

For each writing question you should:
  ☑ write in paragraphs
  ☑ plan one point per paragraph
  ☑ use connectives to guide your reader through the text.

Sample answer

One of the most popular things you can do on the internet is social networking. You can go on websites like Facebook and keep in touch with all your friends. You can also use online encyclopedias to find out about anything you want to know. You can also use the internet to save your photos and share them with your friends and relatives on websites like Facebook, which links back to what I was saying before.

✓ A clear point supported with evidence.

✗ This evidence should be supported with a persuasive explanation.

✗ Avoid phrases like 'links back to what I was saying before'. Instead, **show** the reader the link by using a connective, e.g. **In addition** or **Furthermore** …

Remember that a new point should mean a new paragraph. Remember also to support your points with evidence or an explanation. This point contains neither.

Improved sample answer

The internet is an amazing invention. Using websites called 'search engines', you can type in what you want to know and it will show you the websites that can tell you the answer. It's simple, so you'll pick it up really easily.

In addition, there are hundreds more things you can do on a computer. For example, you can email people and tell them your news or send them your photos. It's much quicker and easier than writing a letter.

✓ Paragraph clearly organised using:
  • point
  • evidence
  • explanation.

Note here the accurate paragraphing, and a connective (In addition) to guide the reader. Note also a connective phrase (For example) to introduce evidence.

Now try this

Write the **first two** or **three** paragraphs of your own answer to the exam-style question above. You could develop some of the ideas from the sample answers, e.g. sharing photos, online encyclopedias or social networking.

EXAM SKILL

Remember to:
  • write in paragraphs
  • use Point-Evidence-Explain to structure each paragraph
  • use connectives to guide your reader through your ideas.

Use this skill to help you improve the quality of your writing.

Getting the right tone

You need to match your language choice and style to the writing task and its audience.

Formal or informal

Most tasks in the Writing section of your exam will require a formal tone, using standard English and formal language choices. Although some tasks may allow a degree of informality – for example, a task aimed at teenagers – beware of using humour. Ask yourself these questions:

- Is it in keeping with the tone of the rest of my writing?
- Does it add to the impact I want to have on the reader?

Point of view

Before you start writing, decide whether you will write in the first person (I) or third person (he, she, they).

- **Writing in the third person** gives your writing authority. It suggests to the reader that the writer's opinion is objective and trustworthy.
- **Writing in the first person** can create a relationship between reader and writer. Use it when writing about a personal experience.

Consistent tenses

You are likely to be writing in either the past or present tense in both writing tasks. Whichever tense you start in, make sure you stick to it throughout.

Present tense:

The Internet (is) a big part of many people's lives. They (use) it to find out information and keep in touch.

Past tense:

The Internet (was) first created in the 1960s. It (was used) by the army in the United States.

EXAM SKILL

Don't change tense midway through a piece of writing, as it is disconcerting for the reader – and it's a sign that you are not in full control of your writing.

> Use this skill to help you improve the quality of your writing.

Worked example

6 'Celebrities have too much influence on our lives.' Write an **article** for your school or college magazine which **persuades** your readers that this statement is right or wrong.
Remember to:
- write an **article**   • use language to **persuade**.   *(24 marks)*

Celebrities have an extraordinary amount of power and influence in our society. I remember once my mate went totally bananas when she heard that her fave singer was opening a shop near where we live. How mental is that? She thought it was like the most important person in the world doing the most amazing thing in the world.

✓ Formal tone, standard English
✗ Sudden and surprising shift into the first person, informal tone.
✗ Informal language / slang

Note how the language becomes less formal in tone. This is inconsistent with the first sentence.

Now try this

Rewrite the 'Sample answer' above, aiming to make the tone more consistent and appropriate throughout.

Remember to have your audience firmly in mind to help you keep a consistent and appropriate tone.

Synonyms

Synonyms are words with similar meanings. Use them to avoid repetition and add variety to your writing.

Using synonyms can make your writing more varied and interesting. Having a range of synonyms for key words and ideas in mind as you write will mean that:

- you don't repeat the same key word throughout your writing
- you can pick the most precise word – the one that really says what you want it to say.

Be your own thesaurus

You know hundreds – perhaps thousands – of words that you rarely use. So you don't need a thesaurus to come up with ambitious, effective vocabulary chosen for its impact. You just need to think through your mental thesaurus. Beware though! Don't use a word if you are not absolutely sure of its precise meaning.

Examples of synonyms

This gives the impression that ...

It seems clear that ...

Comments on evidence often involve the phrase This suggests ... Replace it with:

This implies ...

In other words ...

notion

point

concept

Arguments are often about ideas. To avoid repeating the word idea, you could use:

opinion

viewpoint

Worked example

6 'Celebrities have too much influence on our lives.' Write an **article** for your school or college magazine which **persuades** your readers that this statement is right or wrong.

Remember to:
- write an **article**
- use language to **persuade**.   *(24 marks)*

The <u>idea</u> of <u>celebrities</u> as perfect role models is not the only misguided <u>idea</u> connected with the world of the <u>celebrity</u>. Some people have the <u>idea</u> that <u>celebrities</u> should be consulted on everything from international politics to haircare.

EXAM SKILL

Using the same word more than once can undo all the hard work you put into an answer, making your ideas seem repetitive and uninteresting.

Use this skill to help you improve the quality of your writing.

Repetition can add pace and rhythm to your writing – but there are too many words being repeated too often here, weakening an otherwise strong paragraph.

Now try this

Rewrite the 'Sample answer' above, replacing the words 'celebrities', 'celebrity' and 'idea' with different synonyms.

Before you start, make a list of all the synonyms you can think of for the word 'celebrity'. You can use a thesaurus if you get stuck.

71

Choosing vocabulary for effect: describe

Choosing the most effective vocabulary can have a significant impact on your writing, especially when you are writing to **describe**.

Don't overdo it

When writing to describe, it is important that you do just that. However, be careful not to overdo it.

Avoid piling on the adjectives and adverbs:

> ✗ The sun's glorious golden rays burst through my gleaming windows, sending shimmering sparkling beams of incandescence dancing around my walls.

Describe what matters – not what doesn't

Don't describe everything. Focus on what matters. For example, if you want to describe a phone call shattering an awkward silence, focus on the relevant detail:

> ✗ The insistent ringtone of the phone suddenly filled the room so I hurried to the low, wooden table on which it sat and picked up the slim black handset, pressing it to my ear.

> ✓ The jangling phone made me jump. I answered it.

The best words

The best description often uses fewer, well-chosen words that **show** the reader, rather than **tell** them. Carefully chosen verbs can be especially effective:

> ✗ He walked across the room with a spring in his step. → ✓ He bounced across the room.

> ✗ He flung open the door and walked quickly into the room. → ✓ He flew into the room.

However, sometimes showing the reader takes more words than telling them. Here are a couple of rules.

Don't name your feelings:

> ✗ I felt really really terrified.

> ✓ I clenched my clammy palms into fists and tried to stop my legs shaking.

Do describe the effect they have on you:

> ✗ It hurt a lot.

> ✓ Pain shot through me like a thunderbolt.

Describing people

Choose just one or two details that will give the reader an impression of a person. For example, two of the details opposite could be used to show the reader that this person is concerned about their appearance. The others tell you very little.

> ✗ Brown hair
> ✗ Brown eyes
> ✗ Glasses
> ✗ Dark trousers
> ✓ Wearing a tie
> ✓ Highly polished shoes

Now try this

Write the opening paragraph of the question below, describing your feelings as you come face-to-face with your fear.

> Describe a time when you faced a fear.

Remember:
- your task is to describe, **not** to tell a story, so focus on describing the situation, your thoughts and feelings
- choose only relevant details to describe
- choose the best words that show the reader how you felt.

Choosing vocabulary for effect: argue and persuade

When writing to argue or persuade, you need to be able to use a wide vocabulary of emotive words and positive and negative language.

Vocabulary for impact

Using emotive language can add impact to your argument. For example, you may think that global warming is a problem. To shock your reader into action, you want to emphasise the problem by choosing a more emotive word:

> If we ignore global warming now, we will soon be facing a ~~problem~~

> catastrophe   disaster   calamity

Add even more power to your sentence by intensifying the emotive word:

> horrific   alarming   terrifying

> we will soon be facing a terrifying catastrophe.

Positive and negative

If you frame your ideas in **positive** or **negative** language you can control your reader's reaction to them. For example,

If you **support** fox hunting, it could be described as: 'A humane method of pest control.'

If you **oppose** fox hunting, it could be described as: 'A cruel and barbaric sport.'

If you are arguing in **support** of typical teenage behaviour, you could point out that: 'Sleep is an essential ingredient for the teenage brain's development.'

Taking the **opposing point of view** you might write: 'Idle teenagers lounge in bed for hours, paralysed by their crippling laziness.'

Connotations

You can influence your reader's reaction by thinking about the connotations of your vocabulary choice. Look at these words. Each one has a similar meaning but carries different associations.

> Six hours of intensive revision can make you

> exhausted.

Suggests extreme, intense tiredness, emphasising how tiring revision can be.

> drained.

Implies revision leaves you weak and empty as though it is physically harming you.

> sleepy.

Sounds childish and mocking, suggesting the writer is not taking the problem seriously.

Now try this

Write an opening paragraph for the exam-style question opposite, focusing on vocabulary to persuade the reader.

> Remember to choose vocabulary for its impact and for its connotations.

6 'School is cruel.' Write an **article** for a magazine of your choice which **persuades** your readers that this statement is right or wrong.
Remember to:
- write an **article**
- use language to **persuade**. *(24 marks)*

Language for effect 1

You can use a range of language techniques to add power and impact to your writing.

Rhetorical questions

Use these in argument or persuasive writing to lead the reader to the answer you want.

There is really only one way to answer these questions:

> Who in their right mind would do such a thing?

> Would you stand by and do nothing if you saw a human being treated like this?

You can also use them in descriptive writing to engage the reader in a situation:

> What was going on?   What should I do?

Contrast

Place two opposing ideas or situations in direct contrast to emphasise the difference.

> You can work hard in a job you hate for the rest of your life ...

> or you can work hard on your GCSEs for a couple of years and get the job you want.

You can also use contrast in descriptive writing to exaggerate a detail: 'Among all the smiling, happy faces there was just one exception: my father's sour-faced, snarling scowl.'

Repetition

Repeating a word or phrase can emphasise a key point or idea in an argument:

> Chasing a helpless animal across open country is cruel. Setting a pack of dogs on a helpless animal is cruel. Watching as the dogs butcher the helpless animal is cruel.

It can also add emphasis to an idea in descriptive writing:

> There is no point in discussing it, there is no point in arguing about it, there is no point in shouting about it. Once my father has made up his mind, it is made up.

Lists

Use a list to suggest a range of ideas in your persuasive writing:

> It's quick, simple, easy and cheap.

> The improvement would be huge: students would learn more, learn faster, be more motivated, enjoy school more and achieve better results.

Use it to suggest range or variety in your descriptive writing.

> Scattered across the carpet were balloons, paper hats, lumps of cake, streamers and torn shreds of wrapping paper.

Now try this

Choose **one** of these questions:

1
> **Describe** your favourite place.

2
> 6   Write an **article** for your school or college magazine **persuading** students to take more exercise.
> Remember to:
> * write an **article**
> * use language to **persuade**.   *(24 marks)*

Write **four** short extracts from your chosen task, using **one** of the language techniques above in each.

EXAM SKILL

Don't use these language devices as a tick list in the exam, aiming to include one of each in both of your answers.

Instead, look for opportunities where they will add to the impact of your ideas.

Use this skill to help you improve the quality of your writing.

Language for effect 2

You can use a range of language techniques to add power and impact to your writing.

Direct address

Talking directly to the reader is persuasive. Using the **second person 'you'** can suggest that your ideas are relevant to their lives. For example:

'**you** can get involved in lots of different ways'

this involves the reader and is much more persuasive than:

'There are many ways to get involved.'

Using the **first person plural 'we'** can create a relationship between you, the writer, and the reader. It suggests that we are all in the same situation, facing the same problems:

'If **we** do nothing, then nothing will change. It is up to us to act and act now.'

Pattern of three

Putting words or phrases in linked groups of three adds rhythm and emphasis to your ideas in all kinds of writing:

It doesn't matter if you're a beginner, an improver, or an expert. It's fun for everyone!

It will benefit the students, the teachers, and the community as a whole.

I approached the front door. My hands were cold, clammy and shaking.

Alliteration

Alliteration can add rhythm and emphasis to your writing. Remember: the alliterative words do not have to be **next** to each other – just **near** each other.

It was a truly terrifying experience.

Combined with other language techniques, alliteration can be particularly engaging and powerful: 'It's fun, fast and furious.'

Emotive language

Use emotive language when you want to influence your reader's emotions.

Emotive language can add impact to persuasive and argument writing:

Testing cosmetics on animals is ~~not very nice~~ barbaric and heartless.

Emotive language can make descriptive writing much more vivid for the reader:

~~I was bleeding.~~ Blood was pouring out of me. It ~~hurt~~ was agony.

Now try this

Choose **one** of these questions:

1   Describe a time when you felt under pressure.

2   **6** The head of your school or college is banning the use of mobile phones. Write a **letter persuading** them to change their mind.   *(24 marks)*

Write **four** short extracts from your chosen task, using **one** of the language techniques above in each.

Language for effect 3

You can use figurative language to create a powerful image in your readers' minds. Similies, metaphors and personification can add power to your writing. Used carefully and sparingly, they can also demonstrate imagination, originality and writing craftsmanship.

Similes

A simile is a comparison, usually using **as** or **like**, suggesting a resemblance between one thing and another. It can be used when writing:

• **to inform**

> When you get it right, skateboarding can be **as exhilarating as a skydive from 30,000 feet.**

• **to persuade**

> Smoking cigarettes **is like a game of Russian roulette** – and the chances are, you'll end up losing.

Personification

Personification is the technique of describing something non-human as if it were human. It can be used when writing:

• **to describe**

> Sunlight **danced** on the water as we headed out to sea.

• **to persuade**

> Smoking is highly addictive and, once the habit has got its hands around your throat, it will not let go.

Metaphor

A metaphor is a direct comparison suggesting a resemblance between one thing and another. It can be used when writing:

• **to argue**

> At night, when there is nothing else to do, **the youth club is a bright light in the darkness**, drawing all the young people of the town through its doors.

• **to describe**

> She stared and stared, **her eyes burning holes in my face**.

Avoiding clichés

While an imaginative and original simile or metaphor can add greatly to your writing, a cliché can destroy the effect. So no matter how hurried you are, **do not** describe someone as:

• cool as a cucumber
• white as a sheet
• blind as a bat

… or any other comparison that your reader will have read hundreds of times before.

Now try this

Choose **one** of these questions:

1
> Describe your ideal home.

2
> **6** Most students are driven to school or college. Write an **article** for your school or college website, **persuading** students to walk or cycle instead.
> *(24 marks)*

Write **three** short extracts from your chosen task, using **one** of the language techniques above in each.

EXAM SKILL

Remember these dos and don'ts.

• Don't try to use one simile, one metaphor and one personification in both of your answers.
• Do look for opportunities where they will add to the impact of your ideas.
• Do avoid clichés and be original.

> Use this skill to help you improve the quality of your writing.

Putting it into practice

Look at the exam-style question below and read the two sample student answers.

Worked example

5 Your local newspaper is organising a writing competition. The topic is 'The biggest mistake of my life'. Write your **entry** for the competition, **describing** a time when you made a mistake. Remember to:

- write a **competition entry**
- use language to **describe**.
(16 marks)

Language choice

In each of your writing tasks you should:

☑ choose language appropriate to your audience

☑ make ambitious and effective vocabulary choices to engage your reader

☑ use a range of language techniques.

Sample answer

The worst mistake I ever made was jumping out of a tree. I was <u>down the park</u> with my friends and they dared me to climb this <u>really tall tree</u>. <u>I was about eight. So I climbed up the tree. I got about a metre up and <u>it felt like I was nearly at the sky</u>. I looked down and realised I hadn't got very far and they were all laughing and shouting and encouraging me to go higher. So I carried on climbing. I went up another metre or so. By now I was really scared.

✗ Language choice too informal for this audience.

✗ Limited description, and unambitious vocabulary choice.

✓ Effective use of figurative language.

Note that although there is some limited (but effective) language choice here, there are also missed opportunities to use really effective language (as you can see in the final sentence).

Improved sample answer

My aunt had come to stay. She seemed to be angry every time I saw her, but on this visit she was furious. <u>She frowned and sniffed and sighed</u> at every word I said. So I decided to bake her a cake. Cake was the only thing that ever cheered her up. She loved it. <u>Cream cake, chocolate cake, fruit cake</u>, any cake would make her smile <u>like a lion looking at a zebra</u>. And that was where the trouble started.

✓ Engaging vocabulary choice.

✓ Effective use of language devices:
- pattern of three
- list
- simile.

Notice how this language choice shows humour as well as being effective.

Now try this

Write the **first two** paragraphs of your answer to the exam-style question above.

Remember to choose and use:
- language appropriate to your audience
- language for effect
- a range of ambitious vocabulary and language features.

Sentence variety 1

Using a range of different sentence types adds variety to your writing and helps keep your readers engaged.

Adding variety

Writing for young children uses a limited range of sentence types:

> Penny went out of the house.
> It was raining.
> Soon she was soaked.
> Penny turned around and went home again.

Effective writing for adults uses a variety of sentence types to hold the reader's interest.

Sentence types

There are four basic types of sentence:
- ☑ simple
- ☑ compound
- ☑ complex
- ☑ minor.

You should use all four in your writing for variety and for effect.

See page 30 — for more on sentence types

Complex sentences

Using the two different kinds of complex sentences will help you hold your reader's attention.

1 **Complex sentences using a subordinating clause.** This is where extra information is added using a connective such as: because, although, after, if, since. The main clause gives the most important information. The subordinating clause adds more detail.

Subordinating clause   Main clause

> •Before I went out, I locked all• the doors.

Main clause   Subordinating clause

> •I locked all the doors before• I went out.

You can usually swap the main and subordinating clauses without changing the meaning of the sentence.

2 **Complex sentences using a relative clause.** This is where extra information is added using one of these **relative pronouns**: that, where, which, whose, who, when.

Main clause   Relative clause, separated from the main clause with commas

> •The last time I saw him, which was over a week ago,• • had ended in disaster.

Main clause   Relative clause, separated from the main clause with commas

> •My best friend, who has never• been good at English, got the highest mark in the class.

Now try this

Write the opening paragraph for this question:

> Describe a place you know well. It could be a room in your house, a street, a town, or somewhere you have visited.

Aim to use at least one of each sentence type:
- a simple sentence
- a compound sentence
- a complex sentence with a subordinating clause
- a complex sentence with a relative clause
- a minor sentence.

Sentence variety 2

Thinking about the first word of your sentences can help you add interest to your writing.

First words

Developing writers often start their sentences in similar ways. Try to start your sentences in different ways to add variety to your writing. You can start with any of these.

Type of word	Examples
A pronoun I, you, he, she, it, we, they, my, your	I turned and started.
An article a, an, the	The glass had disappeared.
A preposition above, behind, between, near, with, etc.	Above me, I heard footsteps.
An -ing word (or present participle) running, hurrying, crawling, smiling, etc.	Edging silently to the door, I went to the stairs and listened.
An adjective slow, quiet, huge, violent, etc.	Sharp, prickling pains crept from my fingertips to my hair.
An adverb alarmingly, painfully, happily, etc.	Gingerly, I put my foot on the first stair.
A connective (subordinating clause + main clause) if, although, because, etc.	Although I knew I was in an empty house, I could not help thinking that I was not alone.

Now try this

Write the **first ten** sentences for the question below:

Describe your most memorable moment at school.

Have a go at:
- using all seven different types of sentence opener in your writing
- using a different word to start each of your sentences.

Sentences for effect

Structuring your sentences in different ways can achieve different effects. Practise using various sentence structures to emphasise your argument.

Longer sentences

Use longer sentences to give your reader more information sharply and concisely. You can add information using subordinating clauses, as the example opposite shows.

Be careful though: if you try to cram too much information into one sentence, you could lose your reader's attention.

Main clause

Subordinating clause

Subordinating clause

> Although the idea of achieving good GCSE results is motivating for many people, some people struggle to get down to work because teenage life has so many distractions.

Shorter sentences

Use shorter sentences to suggest pace to the reader:

> I get up. I eat breakfast. I clean my teeth. I throw on some clothes and throw myself out of the front door. I'm ready for school.

Use shorter sentences to create a feeling of tension in the reader:

> The wind howled. The rain poured down. I ran through the night. Every shadow seemed to hide something horrible. Every sound set my heartbeat racing.

The long and the short

Short punchy sentences can be particularly effective: they add impact to an argument, and surprise or tension to a description. Look at the contrast opposite.

Short sentences are particularly effective when they follow a longer sentence.

Long sentence to contrast with a short sentence to surprise.

> Some people believe in leaping out of bed as the sun is rising and settling down to an hour's revision before breakfast, then a couple of hours' more revision before a short jog to revive the brain and another couple of hours' revision before lunchtime. I do not.

Now try this

Write **one** or **two** paragraphs in response to this exam-style question:

> **6** Write an **article** for your school or college website, **persuading** students to play more sport.
>
> Remember to:
> • write an **article**
> • use language to **persuade**.   (24 marks)

Aim to include examples of:
• a series of short sentences to create pace or tension
• a long sentence followed by a short sentence.

Putting it into practice

Look at the exam-style question below and read the two sample student answers.

Worked example

6 'Many people believe that it is important to follow fashion and look good.'

Write an **article** for a teenage website which argues for or against this idea.

Remember to:
- write an **article**
- use language to **argue**.   *(24 marks)*

Sentence variety

In both writing tasks you should:
- ✓ use a range of sentence structures
- ✓ start your sentences in different ways
- ✓ structure your sentences for effect.

Sample answer

Fashion is important because people judge you on how you look, even though you shouldn't it's difficult not to. Fashion can also be fun because shopping and choosing clothes and seeing what your friends are wearing is really enjoyable. Fashion is also something to talk about and do with your friends because if all your friends are in fashion and like the same fashion then you can swap clothes and tell them how they look.

Notice that:
- each sentence starts in the same way
- each sentence follows the same structure
- sentences are all long and complex, using multiple clauses.

To improve your answer you should add variety.

✗ Vocabulary is frequently repeated.

✗ A limited range of connectives creates repetitive vocabulary and sentence structure.

Improved sample answer

How we look is important. It matters. We judge other people by how they look and we expect them to do the same. Otherwise, why do we spend so much time, trouble and money making ourselves look good?

The problem is that sometimes we judge people who cannot help the way they look, either because of how they were born or because of something that has happened to them. This is very wrong.

Notice how the sentences in this answer:
- vary in length
- start with a range of different words.

✓ Two short sentences make a powerful opening statement.

✓ Long sentence, followed by powerful short sentence.

Now try this

Write the **first two** paragraphs of your answer to the exam-style question above.

Remember to:
- use a range of sentence types and lengths
- start sentences in a variety of ways
- structure sentences for effect.

Full stops, question marks and exclamation marks

Failing to use **full stops, question marks, exclamation marks** and **capital letters** correctly can seriously affect the quality of your writing.

Check your full stops

Most students know that a sentence should start with a capital letter and end with a full stop. However, some students do not always remember to check their punctuation. No matter how strong the rest of your writing skills are, poor punctuation – and full stops in particular – will lose you valuable marks. The most common error is using a comma to join two sentences instead of a full stop to separate them. This is called a **comma splice**.

The comma splice

When you want to tell the reader two pieces of information you can do two things.

✓ Separate them with a full stop:

> Puppies are small and cuddly. People do not seem to realise that they will soon grow.

✓ Join them with a connective:

> Puppies are small and cuddly **but** people do not seem to realise that they will soon grow.

✗ You **cannot** join them with a comma:

> Puppies are small and cuddly, people do not seem to realise that they will soon grow.

Question marks

Always check you have put a question mark at the end of a question – especially a rhetorical question.

Exclamation marks

Be **very** careful in your use of exclamation marks. Follow these golden rules.

- Only use an exclamation mark for an exclamation, e.g. 'Thank goodness!' he cried.
- Use them very sparingly. Don't scatter them randomly throughout your writing, and never put one at the end of a title.
- Never use two or more exclamation marks in a row.

Now try this

Rewrite this student's answer, removing all the comma splices. Try to do this in three different ways by:
- adding connectives
- restructuring some of the sentences
- replacing the comma splices with full stops.

Remember that you do not use a comma to join two pieces of information in a sentence. Use a full stop to separate them, or a connective to join them.

Puppies are small and cuddly, people do not seem to realise they will soon grow, after a year or more they are puppies no longer, they have grown into huge dogs needing vast amounts of exercise, vast amounts of food and vast amounts of attention. All too often the result is disaster, it's not just furniture that gets chewed and destroyed, worst of all people can be hurt by dogs that have become aggressive through lack of training or lack of care. Before you buy a puppy, make sure you have spent some time with an adult of the same breed, it could save you a lot of time, trouble and heartache.

Commas

Your answers should show a **range** of punctuation, used **accurately**.

Commas and subordinating clauses

In a complex sentence, the main clause and the subordinating clause can usually be swapped around without changing the meaning of the sentence:

See pages
30 and 78

for more on complex sentences

I meet new people wherever I go. — main clause — subordinating clause

If you begin a complex sentence with the main clause, there is no need for a comma to separate the clauses.

Wherever I go, I meet new people. — subordinating clause — main clause

If you begin a complex sentence with the subordinating clause, use a comma to separate it from the main clause.

Commas and relative clauses

You can add a relative clause to a sentence, giving additional information linked with one of these relative pronouns:

- that
- whose
- where
- who
- which
- when

You should always separate the relative clause from the main clause with commas.

Main clause   Relative clause

The house, which I had never visited before, seemed strangely familiar.

Notice how the clauses have been separated with commas.

Commas in a list

If you are writing a list, add a comma after each word or phrase – apart from the words or phrases which are linked using and.

- Use commas in lists of adjectives:

He was tall, smartly dressed and elegant.

Comma here to separate two items in a list.

No comma here because they are linked with and.

- Use commas in lists of phrases:

There was mud on the floor, mud on the walls, mud on the windows and mud on the ceiling.

Now try this

Look at this exam-style question:

6 'Your school days are the happiest days of your life.' Write an **article arguing** for or against this point of view.
   Remember to:
   - write an **article**
   - use language to **argue**.   (24 marks)

Write **three** to **five** sentences, using commas correctly to separate:
- items in a list
- a main and subordinating clause
- a main and relative clause.

Apostrophes and speech punctuation

Missing or incorrect **apostrophes** and **speech punctuation** are common errors. Make sure you know how to avoid making mistakes with them.

Apostrophes in contractions

When two words are shortened or abbreviated, some letters are missed out or omitted. You should use an apostrophe to show where these letters are missing:

cannot → **can't**
do not → **don't**
I will → **I'll**
let us → **let's**

Abbreviations such as **don't** and **can't** are more informal than the full, unabbreviated versions. Think about your audience when deciding which to use.

Apostrophes of possession

Apostrophes can be used to show that something or someone belongs to someone or something else.

- The boy's hands ...
- Betty's sister ...
- The dog's collar ...
- The school's head teacher ...

Note that if the word to which you are adding the apostrophe ends in s you can just add the apostrophe after the s:

The teachers' voices   Mrs Roberts' book

Note that this is a plural: there is more than one teacher.

You can also, when a name ends in s, add an apostrophe and another s:

Mrs Roberts's book

Speech punctuation

- Use speech marks to enclose the words that are spoken.
- Start the speech with a capital letter.
- There is **always** a punctuation mark just before the closing speech marks.
- Use a comma if you are adding who is speaking ...
- ... followed by a lower case letter immediately after the closing speech marks.
- Use a full stop if you are not adding who is speaking.

'Mum, can I have some sweets?' begged Aran.

'Mum, I want some sweets.'

'It's nearly dinner time,' his mother replied.

'I've just told you,' said his mother patiently.

Now try this

There are **13** punctuation errors in this student's writing. Copy and correct it.

'theres nothing I can do said Garys dad.

'are you sure,' Replied Gary.

'idont know what you mean.' Said his dad.

'i think you do'

Colons, semi-colons, dashes, brackets and ellipses

Using punctuation like **colons** and **semi-colons** helps you develop your ideas and express yourself clearly.

Semi-colons

You can use semi-colons to link two connected ideas instead of using a connective.

For example, you could write:

> The value of education is enormous and it should be treasured.

Or you could write:

> The value of education is enormous; it should be treasured.

Colons

Use a colon to:

- introduce an example

> Students have two choices: work hard or fail.

- introduce a list

> You will need: a pen, a pencil, a ruler, and an eraser.

- introduce an explanation

> English is my favourite subject: I love learning about punctuation.

Dashes and brackets

These can be used to add extra, but not entirely necessary, information to a sentence.

> Before using brackets or dashes, ask yourself: Is this important information? Or would my writing be better without it?

- Dashes can be used in pairs to add information in mid-sentence:

> Several years earlier – though I can't remember when exactly – my grandmother had moved to a remote island off the coast of Scotland.

- One dash can also be used at the end of a sentence, to add information after a pause:

> I'm sure there was a reason – but no one ever told me what it was.

- Brackets must be used in **pairs**:

> The house (which my mother hated and my father loved) was about a mile from the sea.

Ellipses

- You can use an ellipsis in dialogue to suggest a dramatic pause or to show someone falling into silence:

> 'I don't know where I …' He looked mystified.

> 'And the winner is …'

- Using an ellipsis to suggest tension in descriptive writing can seem clichéd. Rely instead on your choice of language and sentence structure to create tension:

> ✗ He opened the door and realised to his horror that the room was completely empty …

> ✓ He opened the door. The room was completely empty.

Putting it into practice

Look at the exam-style question below and read the two sample student answers.

Worked example

5 Your school or college magazine is publishing a series of articles with the title, 'I couldn't live without …' Write your **article**, for the magazine **explaining** what you could not live without and why it is so important to you. It could be an object, a hobby or interest, a person, or even an idea.

Remember to:
• write an **article**
• use language to **explain**.   *(16 marks)*

Punctuation
In both writing tasks you should:
☑ punctuate accurately
☑ use a range of punctuation.

Sample answer

I could'nt live without football, its something I've always loved. I love playing it and watching it whether its a few friends having a kickabout at lunchtime or an FA Cup final on the telly. There are lots of reasons it means so much to me. One is that my dad loves football so its something we have in common. He does'nt play football but we can spend hours talking about it, who scored, who didnt score who should be playing and who should be dropped.

✗ Incorrectly placed apostrophes.

✗ Comma splice. This should either be a semi-colon or a full stop followed by a new sentence.

✗ Missing apostrophe.

✗ Missed opportunity for a colon to introduce a list.

✗ Missing comma separating items in a list.

Note that the use of full stops in the first answer is **generally** accurate, but the full stops in the improved answer are **completely** accurate.

Improved sample answer

I couldn't live without football; its something I've always loved. I love playing it and watching it whether it's a few friends having a kickabout at lunchtime or an FA Cup final on the telly. There are lots of reasons it means so much to me. One is that my dad loves football so it's something we have in common. He doesn't play football but we can spend hours talking about it: who scored, who didn't score, who should be playing and who should be dropped – though I'm not sure he knows what he's talking about.

✓ Correctly placed apostrophe.

✓ Effective use of a semi-colon.

✓ Colon to introduce a list.

✓ Comma separating items in a list.

Dashes like these are used to add additional information.

Now try this

Write the first paragraph of your answer to the exam-style question above. Aim to use a range of punctuation accurately, including commas and apostrophes.

Always remember to check your punctuation – especially full stops – for accuracy.

Common spelling errors 1

There are some spelling mistakes that occur again and again in students' exam responses. You should learn how to avoid making them.

Would have, could have, should have

Students often use **would of** or **should of** or **could of** when they should use **would have, should have,** or **could have**. For example:

> ✗ Global warming could of been prevented. We should of started thinking more carefully about the environment long ago.

This is what should have been written:
could **have** ✓   should **have** ✓

Our, are

Students often confuse **our** and **are**:
- **our** means **belonging to us**
- **are** is from the verb **to be**.

> ✗ We should always look after are bodies. They our precious.

This is what should have been written:
our bodies ✓   are precious ✓

There, their, they're

Make sure you learn these spellings:
- **their** means belonging to **them**
- **there** is used to describe the position of something (**It's over there**) and in the phrases **There is** or **There are**
- **they're** is an abbreviation of **they are**.

> ✗ Their were three people at the table, all eating there dinner.

> ✓ ~~Their~~/There were three people at the table, all eating ~~there~~/their dinner.

Affect, effect

One of these is a verb, and the other a noun:
affect is a verb
effect is usually used as a noun.
So, for example, you may have been **affected** by a problem. But the problem had an **effect** on you. If the word has got **an** or **the** in front of it, it's a noun, so it's spelt **effect**.

Remember: don't be afraid to use an effective word because you're not sure about the spelling.

-ly or -ley?

When you add **-ly** to a word, make sure you don't swap the 'l' and the 'e':

definite + ly = definitely

bravley ✗ bravely ✓
safley ✗ safely ✓
rudley ✗ rudely ✓

There are **very few** words which end in -ley. Learn these examples: alley, medley, trolley, valley.

Its or it's?

It's is an abbreviation of **it is**. **Its** means belonging to **it**.

> ✗ Its the end of it's life.

> ✓ ~~Its~~/It's the end of ~~it's~~/its life.

Now try this

Look back at the last five pieces of writing you have completed. Have you made any of these common spelling errors? If so, correct them.

Common spelling errors 2

Spend some time studying common spelling mistakes so that you don't make them in your exam.

Your and you're

Learn the difference between these two words:
- **your** means **belonging to you**
- **you're** is an abbreviation of **you are**.

> ✗ Your having the time of you're life.

> ✓ ~~Your~~[You're having the time of ~~you're~~[your life.

> Remember: **A lot** is two words. **Alot of people love chocolate** is wrong, but **A lot of people love chocolate** is correct.

We're, wear, were and where

Make sure you are familiar with each of these:
- **we're** is an abbreviation of **we are**
- **wear** is a verb referring to clothing – e.g. **What are you wearing tonight?**
- **were** is the past tense of are – e.g. **they are**, they were
- **where** is a question word referring to place – e.g. **Where are we going?**

> ✗ Wear we're you? Were leaving now.

> ✓ ~~Wear we're~~[Where were you? ~~Were~~[We're leaving now.

Two, too, to

Getting these words wrong is quite a common error:
- **to** indicates place, direction or position – e.g. **I went to Spain.**
- **too** means **also** or an **excessive amount** – e.g. **I went too far.**
- **two** is a number.

> ✗ It's to difficult to get too the highest level.

> ✓ It's ~~to~~[too difficult to get ~~too~~[to the highest level.

Of, off

The easiest way to remember the difference is by listening to the sound of the word you want to use:
- **of** is pronounced ov
- **off** rhymes with cough.

> ✗ He jumped of the top off the wall.

> ✓ He jumped ~~of~~[off the top ~~off~~[of the wall.

Past, passed

Aim to get these two right:
- **passed** is the past tense of the verb to pass – e.g. **He passed all his GCSEs.**
- **past** refers to time that has gone by, or **position** – e.g. **That's all in the past; He ran past the school.**

> ✗ She past out at ten passed six.

> ✓ She ~~past~~[passed out at ten ~~passed~~[past six.

Who's and whose

Whose is a question word referring to belonging, e.g. **Whose book is this?**
Who's is an abbreviation of **who is**.

> ✗ Whose wearing who's coat?

> ✓ ~~Whose~~[Who's wearing ~~who's~~[whose coat?

Now try this

Look back at the last five pieces of writing you have completed. Have you made any of these common spelling errors? If so, correct them.

Common spelling errors 3

Some of the most frequently misspelt are listed below. Make sure you learn how to spell these words properly.

amus**e**ment
arg**u**ment

Notice the 'e' here but not here.

opportunity   difficult
disappoint   disappear
embarrassing   possession
beginning   recommend
occasionally

privilege
definitely
separately
conscious
conscience
experience
independence

Look closely at the vowels – 'e', 'i' or 'a'.

Check which letters are **doubled** and which are not.

bus**i**ness

Silent 'i' in the middle.

believe   weird

'ei' or 'ie'?

rhythm

Two 'h's, but no vowels.

decision

Get the 'c' and the 's' round the right way.

grateful

Not greatful; **grat**eful = to show **grat**itude.

Learning correct spellings

Find a hidden word. Look for words hidden within the word you are learning. For example, **separate** becomes much easier to remember when you notice that there's a rat in the middle of it:

sep a **rat** e

Say what you see. Say the word aloud, breaking it up into syllables and pronouncing them as they are written. For example, read these syllables aloud:

def / in / ite / ly

Now try this

Test yourself on these spellings. Learn any which you get wrong, then you could ask a friend or family member to re-test you.

Proofreading

It is essential that you leave time at the end of the exam to check your work. It could make all the difference.

What kinds of mistakes do you make?

Here's a list of common errors:

- spelling mistakes
- missing or incorrect punctuation
- grammatical errors such as misused, repeated or missing words.

> Most people make **all three** kinds of mistakes, especially when they are writing in a hurry.

Ideally, you should check your work through three times:

- once for spelling
- once for punctuation
- once to check it makes clear sense, with no misused, repeated or missing words.

> You **will** have made mistakes. Aim to find **five or more** in each of your answers.

Alarm bells

Train your proofreading brain to ring an alarm bell whenever you come across **their, there, its, it's** or any one of the common spelling errors that everyone makes. When the alarm rings, **stop!** Double check that you've used the correct spelling.

How to check your spelling

If you know you've spelt a word incorrectly, but you're not sure of the correct spelling, try it three or four different ways in the margin. Pick the one that looks right:

seperatly	separetly
separately ✓	separatley

Reading your work backwards – from bottom to top, right to left – stops you thinking about the meaning of your writing and makes you focus on spelling.

Checking for sense: tips

1 When you are checking for sense, try to read 'aloud inside your head' imagining you can hear your voice.

2 Remember to leave time to check your work at the end of the exam. If you check each answer as soon as you've finished writing it, you'll see what you **think** you wrote, not what you **actually** wrote.

3 If you come across a sentence which is clumsy, doesn't make sense, or both... cross it out and try expressing it in a different way.

Putting it right

Accurate writing achieves higher marks than neat writing. So, if you find a mistake – whether it's a word, a sentence, or a whole paragraph – **cross it out**. Put **one neat line** through the mistake and add your correction by:

to guide the reader
- using one of these / ~~to make a mistake~~
- or by using an asterisk.*

> If you forget to start a new paragraph, use // to mark where one paragraph ends and the next one begins.

* To tell the reader to read this bit next.

Now try this

Look over five pieces of writing you have produced recently. How many mistakes can you find?

Putting it into practice

Look at the exam-style question below and read the two sample student answers.

Worked example

6 'Every teenager should have a part-time job. It teaches them the value of money and prepares them for life.'

Write an **article** for a magazine of your choice, **arguing** for or against this view.

Remember to:
- write an **article**
- use language to **argue**.   (24 marks)

Proofreading

For both your writing tasks you should:
- ☑ spend about 3–5 minutes carefully checking your work
- ☑ correct any spelling errors
- ☑ correct any punctuation errors
- ☑ ensure your writing makes clear sense.

Finding and changing errors could really improve your answer.

Sample answer

Everyone says GCSEs have got easier but they dont realise how difficult they are and how much work we have to do at school. There just isn't time to do all the school work and have a part-time job, we need some to rest and and enjoy ourselves. On an avarage day I go to school for six hours, get home and do an hour or two of homework. I could go out to work in the evenings but Id get home late and be realy tired at school the next day which would make it realy dificult to concentrate at school the next day.

Make sure you spend some time checking your answers. The second sentence:
- is clumsily written
- has errors
- is not clear in its meaning.

✗ Spelling errors

✗ Punctuation errors

Improved sample answer

Working for my money has certainly taught me its value. For example, when I was younger and wanted to buy something, I had to pester my mum.* Now, because I've e→ᵃrned my money, ~~I can buy what I want. Because of that I always make sure I know I want what I'm buying.~~ I make very sure I'm not wasting my money on something I ~~dont~~→don't really need.

* Usually, once I'd got it, I would realise that I didn't really want it anymore.

✓ Spelling and punctuation errors both corrected.

It's fine to cross out clumsy writing and add in something that is easier to read and understand.

✓ The additional explanation effectively reinforces the argument.

Now try this

Look back at a piece of writing you have completed recently. Check it **three** times, looking for:
- sentences that are clumsily written or unclear
- missing or repeated words
- spelling mistakes
- punctuation errors.

Aim to find at least **five** mistakes and correct them.

Answers

SECTION A: READING

1 Questions 1 and 2

1 Retrieve, understand and interpret information from the text.
2 Understand and interpret meaning in the text.

2 Questions 3 and 4

1 The effectiveness of language.
2 Write about presentational features and compare texts.

3 Planning your time in the exam

Q1(b): 6 minutes
Q2: 12 minutes
Q3: 18 minutes
Q4: 18 minutes

4 Reading the questions

- Source 1 and Source 3.
- *compare, presentational, features, effect*
- Presentation
- Remember to:
  write about the way the sources are presented
  explain the effect of the presentational features
  compare the way they look.
- 12 marks
- 18 minutes

5 Approaching the exam paper

1 Q3: 18 minutes (9.39–9.57am)
  Q4: 18 minutes (9.57–10.15am)
2 Q2: Source 2, what made Shane Ridley want to become a computer game designer, explain own words, support.
  Q3: Source 3, language, describe, persuade, explain effects.
  Q4: Sources 1 and 3, compare presentational features, way presented, effect the way they look.

6 Skimming for the main idea

For example: Adults and young people can work together to put an end to cyberbullying.

7 Annotating the sources

Key points could include:
- 'extraordinarily dedicated'
- '£100 a week'
- 'Training is torture'
- 'callused and blistered'
- 'next to no chance of winning medals'.

8 Selecting information

Key points could include:
- Collins is 'a bit of a mystery'
- she is married to a TV actor
- she doesn't do publicity
- she hasn't even met her UK publishers.

9 Purpose and audience

Key points could include:
- focuses on beauty, comfort and relaxation, appealing to adult audience
- persuasive language: 'great ... true ... live long in the memory'.

10/11 Putting it into practice

Answers should include one further point. Here are some examples.
- Improvement in achievement is more closely linked to effort than to ability.
- Students who enjoy school achieve better results.
- Schools can improve enjoyment by improving the 'behavioural climate'.
- A good primary school contributes to success in Maths and Science at secondary school.

12 The writer's viewpoint

Key points could include these.
- The writer is concerned at the use of animal testing around the world.
- The list of countries suggests the issue is widespread.
- The list of examples of animal cruelty is to shock the reader.
- Use of dramatic, emotive language, e.g. 'forced ... kill'.

13 Fact, opinion and expert evidence

Fact: James is 13.
Opinion: James was lucky.
Expert evidence: '"They believe there is nothing else out there," says Mr Mitchell.'

14 Inference

Answers could include these.
- Rozov is 'famous the world over'.
- Rozov has completed several dangerous jumps.
- Rozov is attempting increasingly dangerous jumps.

15 Point-Evidence-Explain

1 For example: The writer uses a stream of negative language to describe Britain. For example, he describes Britain as 'sleazy'. This suggests that Britain is rundown, dirty and immoral.
2 Effective sentences should use connecting phrases to link students' P-E-E.

16/17 Putting it into practice

Answers should include at least three points, and could include the following.
- Mills had always wanted to 'do radio'.
- He was shy and nervous when he was young: he got his nan to ring about the job.
- He thought he wasn't confident enough to be a presenter.
- His first on-air experience was doing the chart rundown.
- He comes from humble beginnings: a small town in Hampshire.

18 Selecting evidence

Answer to be structured using P-E-E and may include some of the points from sample answers.

19 Embedding quotations

For example: The writer fills the article with positive language, suggesting that athletes can 'inspire' young people, giving them 'self-respect' and making them more 'healthy' and 'motivated'. This range of language suggests that sporting role models can have an enormously and entirely positive impact on young people in many different ways.

20 Develop your explanations

For example:
- 'I leap' suggests Grylls' energy and recklessness
- 'This is my world' suggests his life revolves around reckless danger and extreme conditions.

21 Word classes

- Descriptive list, using many adjectives creates a vivid visual image.
- Present participles (-ing words) of action verbs create a strong sense of movement and noise.

22/23 Putting it into practice

For example:
- she was classed as 'stupid and lazy'
- she believed she was stupid and had very low self-esteem
- teachers and other students picked on her
- she had no friends
- she worried her husband would leave her if he found out she was illiterate
- she could not help her children learn to read.

24 Connotations

1 'lowing herd' suggests a group of noisy animals, implying that they do not think or express themselves intelligently as individuals.
2 The writer has no respect for them.

25 Rhetorical devices 1

Answers could include these.
- alliteration for emphasis: 'a hub for half the globe', 'fluctuating fortunes'
- repetition for emphasis: '**any**thing you could not buy there or **any**one'
- repetition to link ideas: 'if **you have not** been there, **you have not** really seen the world'
- pattern of three suggests range and variety: 'drugs, late-night noise and multi-culturalism run riot', 'refuge, or fame, or fortune'.

26 Rhetorical devices 2

Answers could include these.
- emotive language/hyperbole to exaggerate the point – 'obsessed'
- alliteration for emphasis – 'fear of failure'
- contrast to highlight difference of 'my generation' and 'our children' and 'Chinese and Indian children'
- pattern of three/repetition to emphasise ambition – 'to earn money, to have good careers, to make something of our lives'.

27 Figurative language

Source 1:
Simile: 'like vast uncut diamonds' suggests size and value.
Metaphor: 'a floating white blanket of ice' suggests it completely covers the sea.

28/29 Putting it into practice

Answers could include these.
Persuade
- 'Accompanied by an Egyptologist' suggests an expert will be on hand to give you lots of background information.
- 'ten escorted excursions' suggests quantity and quality of excursions.
- Layout highlights savings, e.g. 'up to £200 per person'.

Inform
- Gives specific prices for extending your holiday: 'combine the bustling city of Cairo with a stay in Luxor from £499'.
- Lists the places you can visit – and what you can see there: 'the treasures of the boy king Tutankhamun in the Egyptian museum'.

30 Identifying sentence types

1 Complex – longer sentence with one part dependent on the other.
2 Compound – contains two or more verbs.
3 Simple – gives on piece of information.
4 Complex – longer sentence with on part dependent on the other.
5 Compound – simple sentences joined by 'and'.
6 Minor – does not contain a verb.

31 Commenting on sentence types

Answers should focus on sentence length and/or structure, commenting on the reasons for the writer's choice, e.g. audience, mood, emphasis, impact, etc.

32 Making the best comments

For example:
Evidence: 'my brain – not the size of my bust – was my ultimate weapon.'
Comments on:
- viewpoint – intelligence is far more important than appearance
- purpose – the writer belittles appearance to convince the reader of the importance of intelligence
- language choice – the alliteration of 'brain' and 'bust' encourages the reader to link and compare their relative value
- sentence structure – the phrase 'not the size of my bust' is separated from the rest of the sentence with dashes, adding emphasis to the writer's dismissal of its importance
- effect on the reader – the belittling phrase 'the size of my bust' creates a humorous tone to engage the reader further.

33 Comment on language and purpose: argue and persuade

Answers to include: rhetorical questions, direct address, emotive language, contrast, lists, repetition – and their effect.

34 Comment on language and purpose: describe

Answers to include: language choice, the five senses, figurative language, feelings – and their effect.

35 Comment on language and purpose: inform and explain

Answers should include: structure, tone, facts and statistics – and their effect.

36/37 Putting it into practice

Points could include these.
Persuade
- Capitalisation and repetition of 'beaches' suggests this beach is special and different.
- Positive, superlative language, e.g. 'world beater', 'perfection'.
- Simile – 'as soft as an eiderdown'.
- The writer emphasises his wealth of experience to influence the reader: 'I've visited a lot of beaches during my hard life as a travel writer'.

Describe
- Simile: 'like icing sugar'.
- Lots of description of colour: yellow, pink, blue, purple.

38 Identifying presentational devices 1

Answers could include:
- dominant colour orange suggests sunny, positive attitude to success
- information/advice summarised in bold headings, some more positive and appealing, e.g. 'Pamper yourself'
- image reflects target audience; hat and sunglasses suggest this information is relevant even to 'cool' teenagers!

39 Identifying presentational devices 2

Answers could include: at least three presentational and structural features, e.g. sections, boxes, bullet points, numbered or lettered lists, tables, paragraphs.

40 Using P-E-E to comment on presentational devices

Key points could include:
- headings give information to engage the reader and highlight the writer's viewpoint
- image illustrates the article; smiling children suggests they are enjoying competition; winning tape suggests emphasis on winning/competition.

41 Commenting on headlines

Key points could include:
- headline – summarises story; alliteration adds impact/ drama; emotive language ('batters')
- subheading – adds further information; use of facts; emotive language ('homeless … torrential … strike').

42 Image and effect

The description of the photo to include what it will show to convince a reader it really was a holiday of a lifetime.

43 Comparing the presentation of two source texts

Further features could include the use of the blue buttons across the top of the Blue Cross website showing visitors how they can help the charity and the use of the subheading in the Help for Heroes poster which uses emotive language 'wounded' to appeal to the reader.

44/45 Putting it into practice

Key points could include:
- shadow covering face like a mask emphasises anonymity and secrecy.

46 Planning to compare presentation

Points on the texts could include the following.
- Both headings are bold to attract attention; Source 1's subheading uses puns; Source 2's heading is purely informative.
- Source 1 image shows the train; Source 2 image shows James May.
- Source 1's text is organised as one block; Source 2 highlights and structures questions and answers using bold text.

47 Answering a compare question

Answers could include any of the points mentioned in the answers to page 46.

48/49 Putting it into practice

Points could include these.
- Source 1 features buttons/text to encourage interaction, e.g. 'Upload your ideas'; Source 2 gives a website address.
- The heading in Source 2 is in capital letters and uses a font suggesting wear/damage reflecting the text of the poster. The headings in Source 1 are highlighted using capitals/different coloured background strips.

SECTION B: WRITING

50 Reading the questions

- Audience: a national newspaper audience of adults/ older teenagers.
- Purpose: describe, explain.
- Form: article.
- Topic: the perfect school.

51 The questions and planning your exam time

- choice of magazine audience; argue; article; TV viewing.
- tourists; persuade; blog; about a local area.

52 Writing for an audience

For example: You may think you've got ages to prepare for your GCSEs. You may think you don't need to worry about them just yet. But time flies and it won't be long before you're sitting in that exam hall. So it's important to start getting ready for them now.
(**Note the use of some informal features**, e.g. abbreviations such as 'you've', which are appropriate to this audience but would not be in a more formal text.)

53 Writing for a purpose: inform and explain

1 Subheadings could include:
- Schoolwork
- Talking to your teenager
- What to do when friends come round
- Hair and clothes
- Bedtime.

2 Tone: an informal tone suggesting a friendly and supportive voice, but using standard English to suggest the information is reliable and trustworthy.

3 Facts and statistics: e.g. research suggests teenagers need more sleep, suffer from mood swings caused by hormonal changes, etc.

54 Writing for a purpose: describe

For example: The dark closed around me as the door clicked shut. I rattled the handle and, as I realised it was locked, a shudder climbed up my spine.

(**Note the use of the senses** (*dark, clicked, rattled*); the physical symptoms of fear (*shudder*); and the use of personification (*climbed*)).

55 Writing for a purpose: argue and persuade

Points + evidence examples:
- could be the beginning of a great career; many international superstars such as Lady Gaga first performed in school talent shows
- could win you some money; the top three acts win cash prizes
- all proceeds go to a great cause; if everyone bought a ticket we could buy a herd of goats for a village in a developing country.

Counter-argument examples:
You might think standing on stage will be embarrassing, but if you perform in a group, you can support each other.

Rhetorical device examples:
- fame, fortune and a fantastic future could be just around the corner. (alliteration/pattern of three)
- what's the worst that can happen? (rhetorical question)
- one minute you're standing on stage, the next you're on top of the world. (metaphor/hyperbole)

56 Putting it into practice

1
- Audience: the head of school/college.
- Form: letter.
- Purpose: argue for or against.
- Topic: sell playing fields, build science block and library.

57 Form: letters and emails

Address; date; name; yours sincerely, yours faithfully; signature.

58 Form: articles

Make sure a key idea is in paragraph 1, more detail in paragraph 2 and a quotation in paragraph 3.

59 Form: information sheets

Make sure there is a heading, some key subheadings and some structural features.

60 Putting it into practice

Key points to consider are:
- language should be formal standard English
- opening paragraph could sum up the reason for writing and outline of your argument
- conclusion could sum up your argument and explain why you feel it is so important, e.g. what would be the consequences of young people volunteering or not volunteering?

61 Planning an answer: describe

Plans should include four or five key ideas and a range of supporting details/language ideas.

62 Planning an answer: inform or explain

Here is a possible structure.
- Paragraph 1: introduction – describe/explain the 'one thing'.
- Paragraph 2: explain how/when you realised it was so important.
- Paragraph 3: explain how it could make a difference to teenage life.
- Paragraph 4: explain how it could make a difference throughout people's entire lives.

63 Planning an answer: argue or persuade

Here is a possible plan.
- Introduction: hundreds of channels, 24 hours a day, television can dominate.
- Point 1: TV can be informative/educational.
- Point 2: shared experience of high quality drama, etc. (no different to theatre but cheaper and more accessible).
- Counter-argument: some say it takes over our lives; they need to learn how to turn it off.
- Conclusion: like anything, TV is good and bad; it depends on how it's used. Used carefully/selectively it can bring people together, entertain, inform and educate.

64 Beginnings

1 For example:
- Do we ever question the purpose of school? Or do we just go there every day because we have to?
- Exam results can affect our future, but the experience of school can change our lives forever.
- Nearly half of 16-year-olds in the UK do not achieve five good passes at GCSE.

2 For example: **Exam results can affect our future, but the experience of school can change our lives forever.** While Year 11 students are constantly subjected to their teachers panicking about looming exams, we should remember how relatively unimportant those exams really are. School does not just teach us enough maths and geography to get a GCSE or two. School helps teach us how to live in the world.

(**Note that the bold opening sentence is developed and justified** in the remainder of the paragraph as the writer's argument is introduced and outlined: exams are unimportant; school teaches us much more than how to pass them.)

65 Endings

For example: It is important to work hard at school, to achieve the best results we can for our own satisfaction – but the lessons we learn about being with other people, about setting goals and working towards them, about co-operation and survival will stay with us forever. School days may not be the happiest days of our lives; but they can teach us how to be healthy and happy with ourselves and each other for the rest of our lives. And isn't that more important than a handful of A*s?

(**Note** the first sentence of this conclusion summarises the writer's argument; the second adds a positive note; the final sentence asks a rhetorical question, further promoting their argument.)

66 Putting it into practice

Effective plans will include:
- ideas for an introduction and conclusion
- a range of key points
- some developed detail for each key point
- key points logically sequenced.

67 Paragraphing

If students choose to add a paragraph to the first example they should use Point-Evidence-Explain.

If they have added a paragraph to the second example they need to have clearly introduced the reader to the content of the paragraph then developed it and added detail.

68 Using connectives

Here are some examples.
- Revision is essential preparation for exams, **therefore / consequently** it is important to plan time for it.
- **Moreover / In addition**, revision can build your confidence.
- **For example**, in a subject **such as** English, confident writers can often produce more effective responses.
- **In particular**, this is true of argument writing **because** the writer must feel sure of their ideas and convey this certainty to the reader.
- **In the same way**, the reader's response will be all the stronger when guided by a confident descriptive writer.
- **However**, the writer's confidence must be based on skill and understanding achieved through careful revision. Self-belief is not enough.

69 Putting it into practice

Effective answers will:
- be structured using Point-Evidence-Explain
- sequence and signal their argument using a range of connectives.

70 Getting the right tone

For example: Celebrities have great power and influence in our society. Some time ago, a famous singer was due to open a shop in our local area. A friend of mine could not contain her excitement. To her it was the most important event of her life. To me this is a worrying sign that she has an unhealthy obsession with celebrity.

71 Synonyms

For example: The idea of celebrities as perfect role models is not the only misguided ~~idea~~concept connected with the world of the ~~celebrity~~ famous. Some people have the ~~idea~~notion that ~~celebrities~~ superstars should be consulted on everything from international politics to haircare.

72 Choosing vocabulary for effect: describe

For example: A bead of sweat trickled down my forehead and ran into my eye. My eyelid flickered, twitching anxiously as it blinked away the pain. I could feel my shirt stuck to the sweat pooling on my back and the tremor in my stomach becoming a violent jolting. It was getting closer.

(**Note** how this response focuses closely on the physical symptoms of the feeling of fear, but does not yet reveal the cause of it, hoping to intrigue the reader.)

73 Choosing vocabulary for effect: argue and persuade

For example: In the UK at this very moment hundreds of children, some as young as five, are being kept in appalling conditions. They are caged for up to seven hours a day. They are often made to sit in silence while adults hurl abuse at them. They are subjected to ruthless punishments. Most shockingly of all, this brutal and barbaric treatment is accepted as normal.

(**Note** the use of negative emotive language – *appalling*, *ruthless*, etc. – to emphasise the paragraph's central idea, and the language chosen for its connotations of imprisonment and torture – *caged*, *brutal*, *barbaric*.)

74 Language for effect 1

2 For example:
- rhetorical question – Do you want to live a long and healthy life?
- contrast – Roaming the great outdoors and breathing lungfuls of fresh air in the sunshine is much more enjoyable than sitting in a stale, airless room staring mindlessly at the television.
- list – Obesity can increase your risk of diabetes, heart attack, depression, arthritis, liver failure and breathing difficulties.
- repetition – Exercise can improve your health. Exercise can improve your happiness. Exercise can change your life.

75 Language for effect 2

2 For example:
- direct address – You would never believe the pressure my mum put on me.
- pattern of three – She nagged, pestered and hounded me for days.
- emotive language – I thought my head was going to explode.
- alliteration – This was going to be the most miserable minute of my entire life.

76 Language for effect 3

2 For example:
- simile – The chandelier shines <u>like the sun</u>.
- metaphor – This room <u>is my desert island</u> – a place where I can have some peace and quiet.
- personification – The huge, soft chair <u>welcomes me with open arms</u>.

77 Putting it into practice

Effective answers should include:
- a range of well chosen and varied vocabulary
- simile, metaphor and personification used **appropriately** and **sparingly**
- a range of language techniques for effect, e.g. repetition, alliteration, etc.

78 Sentence variety 1

For example:
- simple – My bedroom is tiny.
- compound – I can just about stand up and raise my arms without touching the walls on either side.
- complex + subordinating clause – If it ever got cleaned, I would have a lovely view of my neighbour's bathroom window.
- complex + relative clause – The window, which is about the size of a postage stamp, is filthy.
- minor – Lovely.

79 Sentence variety 2

For example:
- pronoun – I was waiting alone in a classroom.
- article – An eerie silence had fallen.
- preposition – Beyond the classroom door, I heard footsteps.
- -*ing* word – Holding my breath, I waited.
- adjective – Empty and cold, the classroom did nothing to comfort me.
- adverb – Slowly I realised there was a man standing in the doorway.
- connective – Although I had never seen him before, I knew immediately why he was there.

80 Sentences for effect

For example: The ball landed at my feet. I started to run. I dodged left. I dodged right. Still the ball was with me. The goal was ahead. I kicked. Almost in slow motion, I watched the ball sail over the heads of three defenders, swerve round the goalkeeper's hands, and fly with a satisfying thump into the net just as the final whistle blew. We'd won.

81 Putting it into practice

Effective answers should:
- use a range of simple, compound, complex and minor sentences
- use a range of sentence lengths
- start sentences in a variety of ways.

82 Full stops, question marks and exclamation marks

For example: Puppies are small and cuddly, **however** people do not seem to realise they will soon grow. **A**fter a year or more they are puppies no longer. They have grown into huge dogs needing vast amounts of exercise, vast amounts of food and vast amounts of attention. All too often the result is disaster – **and** it's not just furniture that gets chewed and destroyed. **W**orst of all people can be hurt by dogs that have become aggressive through lack of training or lack of care. Before you buy a puppy, make sure you have spent some time with an adult of the same breed. It could save you a lot of time, trouble and heartache.

83 Commas

For example:
- a list – Nursery school, primary school, middle school and secondary school make up a large proportion of our early lives.
- main + subordinating clause – Although there may be difficult moments, the friendships we make at school can last a lifetime.
- main + relative clause – Those difficult moments, which seem terrible at the time, are easily outnumbered by the happy ones.

84 Apostrophes and speech punctuation

The corrections are shown in bold.
'There's nothing I can do,' said Gary's dad.
'**A**re you sure?' replied Gary.
'**I** don't know what you mean,' **s**aid his dad.
'**I** think you do.'

86 Putting it into practice

Effective answers should include a range of accurate punctuation including commas, apostrophes, colons and semi-colons.

87 Common spelling errors 1

Are students spotting all their spelling mistakes?

88 Common spelling errors 2

Are students spotting all their spelling mistakes?

89 Common spelling errors 3

Are students using effective strategies to learn words?

90 Proofreading

Are students spotting errors in their writing?

91 Putting it into practice

Effective answers should contain at least five corrected mistakes.

There are no questions printed on this page.

There are no questions printed on this page.

There are no questions printed on this page.